Lydgate and Burgh's
Secrees of old Philisoffres.

Early English Text Society.
Extra Series, LXVI.

BERLIN: ASHER & CO., 13, UNTER DEN LINDEN.
NEW YORK: C. SCRIBNER & CO.; LEYPOLDT & HOLT.
PHILADELPHIA: J. B. LIPPINCOTT & CO.

Lydgate and Burgh's
Secrees of old Philisoffres.

A VERSION OF THE 'SECRETA SECRETORUM.'

EDITED FROM THE SLOANE MS. 2464,

with Introduction, Notes, and Glossary,

BY

ROBERT STEELE.

LONDON:
PUBLISHT FOR THE EARLY ENGLISH TEXT SOCIETY
BY KEGAN PAUL, TRENCH, TRÜBNER & CO.,
PATERNOSTER HOUSE, CHARING-CROSS ROAD.

UNIVERSITY PRESS

Great Clarendon Street, Oxford OX2 6DP
United Kingdom

Oxford University Press is a department of the University of Oxford.
It furthers the University's objective of excellence in research, scholarship,
and education by publishing worldwide. Oxford is a registered trade mark of
Oxford University Press in the UK and in certain other countries

© The Early English Text Society 1894

The moral rights of the authors have been asserted

Database right Oxford University Press (maker)

First Edition published in 1894

All rights reserved. No part of this publication may be reproduced,
stored in a retrieval system, or transmitted, in any form or by any means,
without the prior permission in writing of Oxford University Press,
or as expressly permitted by law, or under terms agreed with the appropriate
reprographics rights organization. Enquiries concerning reproduction
outside the scope of the above should be sent to the Rights Department,
Oxford University Press, at the address above

You must not circulate this book in any other form
and you must impose this same condition on any acquirer

Published in the United States of America by Oxford University Press
198 Madison Avenue, New York, NY 10016, United States of America

British Library Cataloguing in Publication Data
Data available

Library of Congress Cataloging in Publication Data
Data available

Extra Series, 66

ISBN 978-0-85-991982-1

CONTENTS.

	PAGE
FOREWORDS	vii
APPENDICES:	
I. Documents relating to Lydgate	xxiii
II. The IX properties of wine, by Lydgate	xxx
III. In praise of Lydgate by Burgh	xxxi
IV. Specimen of MS. Add. 14408	xxxiii

LYDGATE AND BURGH'S 'SECREES OF OLD PHILISOFFRES'

1. The Prolog 1
2. here is the fourme of the Epistil that kyng Alysaundre sent to his maister Aristotiles 5
3. Thanswere of Aristotilees 6
4. This Rubryssh rehersith name of the philisoffre Callid philip, born in parys, which was translator of this book 7
5. here the Translator resortith ageyn to set in a prologe, on this wyse 10
6. here folowith the secund pistil that kyng Alysaundre sent to his maistir Aristotiles 15
7. To telle of hym the Genealogie which translated this book 19
8. Here is the Epistil of the translator 20
9. Of foure maner kynges diuers of disposicion 23
10. How Aristotil declarith to kyng Alisaundre of the stoonys 31
11. how kyng Alisaundre must prudently Aforn conceyve in his providence 32
12. how witt of Sapience or of discrecioun may be parceyvid in a kyng or a prynce 33
13. how a kyng shuld be Religious 34
14. how a kyng shulde be arrayed lych his Estat 34
15. how this vertu Chastite apperteyneth wel in a kyng ... 34
16. how it longith to a kyng oonys in the yeer to shewe hym in his Estat Royal 35
17. Of his dewe observaunce that longith to a kyng 35
18. how solace and disport longith to a kyng 36
19. What apparteynyth also to his glorye 36
20. The Similitude of a Kyng 36
21. how a kyng shulde be gouernyd in al maner of wedrys ... 36

Contents.

CHAPTER	PAGE
22. how a kyng shuld be mercyable	37
23. It longith to a kyng specially to kepe his promys	37
24. how stodye & clergye shuld be promotyd in a kyngdome	37
25. how a kyng hovith to haue a leche to kepe his body	38
26. how a kyng shuld be gouernyd in Astronomye	39
27. Next folowith the vtilite of the helthe of a kyng	39
28. how mechil a-vayl is comprehendid in the diligence of a good leche	39
29. A special Epistil to the Singuleer helthe of a prynce	40
30. To conserve hele aftir a mannys Complexion	40
31. how a kyng must take keep whan he shal reste and whan he shal sleep	40
32. how a leche shal gouerne a prynce slepyng & wakyng	41
33. Of the foure sesouns of þe yeer I gynne at veer	42
34. Next than folowith the sesoun Callid Estas	43
35. Thanne folowith after the Thridde sesoun callid Autumpne	45
36. The fourthe determynacioun of the foure sesouns of the yeer	46
37. here deyed this translator and nobil poete: and the yonge folowere gan his prologe on this wyse	48
38. how a kyng shal conserve natural hete & helthe of body	51
39. Aristotil writ in A pistil to Alisaundre which hurt the body	52
40. how the body is devided into foure principal parties	53
41. The secund principal part of the body	54
42. The Thrydde principal party of the body	55
43. The fourthe principal parte of the body	56
44. An Ensample how a kyng shulde be inquisitiff to knowe diuers Oppynyouns of lechis or of phisiciens	57
45. How profitable is to knowe diuersite & kyndes of metes & drynkes	58
46. The knowyng of watrys, and which be moost profitable	59
47. Of knowynges of vynes, & noynges & bountes of them	61
48. Here specially preyseth wyn, and techith a medycyn ageyn drounkenesse of it	63
49. Of the Rightwisnesse of a Kyng and of his Counseil	64
50. Of a kynges Secretary	73
51. What a kynges massageer oughte to bee	74
52. Of Equiperacioun of Sogettys and Conservacioun of Justice	75
53. Of the governaunce of Batayle	76
54. Of the Crafft of physynomye, and the ymage of ypocras	78
NOTES	87
GLOSSARY	119

FOREWORDS.

§ i. *The Interest of the Poem,* p. vii.
§ ii. *Authorship of the 'Secreta Secretorum,'* p. vii.
§ iii. *Arabic Texts,* p. viii.
§ iv. *The* 1*st Latin Translation,* p. ix.
§ v. *The* 2*nd Latin Translation,* p. x.
§ vi. *The printed Latin Text, and the Versions,* p. xi.
§ vii. *Works founded on the 'Secreta Secretorum,'* p. xii.
§ viii. *The 'Secreta Secretorum' in English,* p. xiii.
§ ix. *The Manuscripts,* p. xiv.
§ x. *The Text used by Lydgate,* p. xv.
§ xi. *Summary of its History,* p. xv.
§ xii. *The Life of Lydgate,* p. xvi.
§ xiii. *The Life of Benedict Burgh,* p. xvii.
§ xiv. *Remarks on the Poem,* p. xviii.
§ xv. *The Metre of the Poem,* p. xviii.
§ xvi. *The Rhyme,* p. xix.
§ xvii. *General Characteristics of Lydgate's Language,* p. xx.
§ xviii. *Concluding Remarks,* p. xxi.

§ i. THE poem, printed for the first time, which the Society offers to the public, has a double interest—as the last work of Lydgate it shows clearly the changes which have come over the language during a life-time devoted to writing—and as a translation of the *Secreta Secretorum* it brings us before one of the key-books of medieval literature.

I have endeavoured in the following pages to give some account of the *Secreta Secretorum* and its history, to summarise what is known of the authors of this translation, and, though relieved of much of the work which would otherwise have fallen upon me by the work of another editor in this series (Dr. Schick), to add some remarks on the language and peculiarities of the poem.

The text printed is that of Sloane 2464. It is the fullest and the earliest copy we possess. No emendation is made without the authority of the other MSS., and these are carefully noted.

§ ii. The *Secreta Secretorum* is attributed to Aristotle, and is said to have been written in answer to the request of Alexander. The prince, absent on an expedition, writes to the philosopher, desiring his presence, with the aim of learning that secret doctrine which the Eastern mind looks for from every teacher. Aristotle unable to go to him, and unwilling either to communicate his doctrine openly, or to disoblige his pupil and patron, writes him a treatise, '*de Regimine Principum,*' intimating at the same time that his secret teaching lies hid there under a veil. The work, as we have it, is doubly divided—into ten books of very unequal length, and into chapters numbered consecutively.

As may be thought, no Greek text corresponding with this work has been found, though certain portions of it have been drawn from Greek sources. The work itself professes to be translated from Greek into Chaldee (which generally means Syriac) and thence into Arabic, and accordingly our earliest texts are Arabic. There are, however, signs of acquaintance with Greek names in the work. A knowledge of the connection between Æsculapius and the sun, and the descent of Aristotle from the Æsculapides are clearly shown by the choice of finding a MS. of Aristotle's dealing with health in a temple dedicated by Æsculapius to the Sun. I may be allowed to suggest too that there may be some connection between the fact that Asclepiades did write on Alexander the Great (Arrian vii. p. 477, Ed. 1668) and this legend. The Syrian origin of our work is rendered probable by the finding of the book at Antioch (l. 443), by the attribution of the astrological chapters to Cyprian (l. 1189), who was a noted magician and a native of the Syrian Antioch in the 3rd century,—afterwards a Christian, Bishop of Carthage, saint, and martyr under Diocletian, and by the fact that Bar Hebraeus (Greg. Abulpharagus), in his Hist. Dynast. VI., Oxon, pp. 56, 86, speaks of a Syriac work of Philemon on Physiognomy—translated from the Greek—and compares him to Hippocrates. Philemon I take to be Polemon, not the Philo quoted by him. I have come upon Greek sources for two different tracts in the work. Caps. xlix—li (l. 1660—1771) are a translation of a letter, "ad valetudinem tuendam," sent by Diocles Caristes (B.C. 320) to Antigonus, which is preserved for us by Paulus Aegineta. (I quote from Lugd. 1589. 8°., p. 109). Lib. X (l. 2465—2723) is founded on the work of Polemon, an early writer on Physiognomy and commentator on Aristotle. He is quoted by Origen (150) *contra Celsum*, I. (Cantab. 1677. 4°., p. 26.) His work is included by Franzius in his *Scriptores Physiognomiæ Veteres*. (Altenburg, 1780. 8°). Hermogenes is Hermes Magnus, the legendary author of all science, but I cannot find the quotations in any of the works attributed to him that I know.

§ iii. *Arabic Texts.* There are two forms of the Arabic text in England, one short, as in the British Museum Add. 7453. 75v° to 76v°., and another longer, as in Bodl. MS. Laud A. 88. I have seen no other MSS. in England, though doubtless many exist, but they abound in foreign libraries. It is especially noteworthy that one of the Vatican MSS. is written in Syriac characters, when we remember that the work is compiled in Syriac from Greek sources, and translated thence by the author.

Its Arabic name is '**sirr alasrar.**' I find it impossible to say, without an actual comparison of several texts, whether the shorter Arabic form is merely a part of the longer, or whether the Arabic text grew, as we shall find the Latin one did. There is some reason for holding the latter view.

Some little difficulty is caused to the student by the fact that two Johns have been translators of this book—a Syrian Christian, and a Spanish physician. I have not endeavoured to make the distinction in the sidenotes, which are intended to represent what was in Lydgate's mind when he wrote, reserving for this introduction any discussion of the matter. We learn from the Arabic that the author of the treatise is Jahja Ibn al Batrik (or John, son of Batrik).[1] Lydgate, following the Latin texts, which confuse him with Johannes Hispalensis, calls him 'John, a spanyol born, ... And Callyd sone / of Oon patricius' (ll. 604, 609).

The author, there can be little doubt, was one of the school of Syriac Christian physicians, so celebrated in the early days of Muhammedan rule. His accuracy (relatively speaking) in dealing with medical matters, his reliance on astrology as a means of diagnosis and prognosis (a tradition brought into Europe at a later period by the school of Salerne), and his inclusion of alchemy and the occult properties of gems as a quite subordinate feature of the treatise—all these point him out as a medical man of the 8th or 9th century.

The prologue (ll. 1—133) and the two letters (134—210) are usually attributed in English works to a later translator of the book into Latin. They are, however, found in the Arabic text, which begins, 'God prosper the Emir-al-Muminim' (the leader of the true believers), as well as in the early Hebrew translation. In the Latin text they are headed, '*The prologue of a certain doctor recommending Aristotle.*'

§ iv. *The first Latin translation.* The Arabic of John, son of Batrik, was first translated into Latin by Johannes Hispalensis for 'Teophina, queen of the Spaniards.'[2] The *Secreta Secretorum* is thus one of the few books which were translated directly from Arabic into Latin, without passing through the Hebrew. I have found his translation in a 14th century MS. in the British Museum (Addit. 26,770), where it occupies two small quarto leaves, and in eight other MSS. there. In the printed editions it is expanded into Caps. xxxiv to xlv, and forms the basis of lines 1261—1491 of our text. It consists of a short treatise on the rules

---

[1] Though the attribution of the translation to him is itself believed to be a disguise of the real compiler.
[2] Who appears in Sloane 405 as Charesie.

§ V. *The Second Latin Translation.*

of health, and of another on the four seasons of the year. In his Introduction, Johannes quotes the Arabic title as 'tursesar,'[1] and speaks of finding the book in the Temple of the Sun, written in letters of gold, and of bearing it home to translate, as in ll. 610—637, but into Latin, not Arabic.

I have been unable to trace 'Teophine' in any of the genealogies of Spanish rulers, but Johannes Hispalensis is well known.[2] He was John Avendeath, a converted Jewish physician, who translated (about 1135—1142) from Arabic into Latin a number of works principally of a medical and astronomical character, and is connected with Spain by the fact that another of his works, a treatise on arithmetic, '*de algorismo*,' was translated for Raimund, Archbishop of Toleto. A monograph on his works will be found in the works of Steinschneider, and an Alchemical tract of Arabic origin bearing his name is found in the Sloane MS. 212.

§ V. *The second Latin translation.* Toward the close of the next century, another translation direct from the Arabic was made by Philip Tripolitanus (or Philip Clericus) enlarging that of Johannes Hispalensis. He used the longer Arabic text, which included, besides the above, the prologue 'in praise of Aristotle,' the letter and answer respecting Persia, the prologue of Jahja Ibn al Batrik, and the chapters on The final intention of kings, Astronomy, Precious stones and talismans, The four parts of the body, The knowledge of foods, waters, and wines, Baths, Venesection, Justice, The choice of officers, secretaries, messengers, and counsellors, and, lastly, on Physiognomy. This translation is dedicated to Guido, a man of Valence, Bishop of Tripoli, or as some copies have it, to Guido de Vere, Bishop and Metropolitan of Valence. Steinschneider in his monograph on the *Secreta Secretorum* (Jahr. f. rom. u. engl. Lit., xii. 4, p. 366) places Guido A.D. 1204, on the strength of an old deed of that year naming G. bishop of Tripoli, but this name has been otherwise ascertained to be Gaufridius. The lists of Bishops give us three bishops of Valence, called Guido (990—995, 1016—1025, 1272—1274), and one bishop of Tripoli in 1279. Förster places him about 1150 or 1210, if he was bishop of Tripoli.

[1] The forms the Arabic words *sirr alasrar* assume will give some idea of the difficulty one meets with in connecting Middle Age Latin forms with their Arabic original. I have found *tuosesar, cirotesar, curoscesca, tymessar, cyretesar, tyralaceare, cyralaurar, dyalicerar, cyralacerar.*

[2] See Bréchillet-Jourdain, "*Recherches sur de Aristotle.*" The reading Charesie (Sl. 405) suggests Tarasia d. of Alfonso VI, king of Leon and Castile, mother of the 1st king of Portugal, who reigned in his place 1112—1128, and died Nov. 1130. It was not unusual to style the daughter of the King of Spain, Queen. The date of this translation would then be 1128—1130, a date confirmed by the preface, which indicates that it is one of his first translations.

§ vi. *The printed Latin Texts, and the Versions.*

The question of date might be attacked in this way; there are two stories in the *Secreta Secretorum*, that of the poison-maiden, and that of the Jew and Muhammedan. If either of these are met with before the thirteenth century, it would seem to follow that the *Secreta* was translated fully at some earlier period. It requires, of course, wide experience to assert a negative, but I believe the former story first appears in the *Gesta Romanorum*,[1] and the latter in Gower.[2] Michael Scot († before 1235) quotes the Sec. Sec. in his Physiognomy, and there is no doubt that Roger Bacon (in 1256) knew parts of the work which were not translated by Johannes Hispalensis, for he quotes part of the second letter of Aristotle, and makes constant references to the work, as well as using the title familiarly in other connections. It was also known to Albertus Magnus (1250).

We may then attribute to the 12th or 13th century this translation, and certain parts of the shorter printed Latin text which have no Arabic original. These are ll. 330—476, 477—602, 638—735 (a distortion of the second letter of Aristotle to Alexander), and 736—973 (Of the four manners of kings touching largesse): which we may attribute to Philip of Tripoli, who was undoubtedly a Frenchman and most probably of Paris, as tradition asserts.

§ vi. *The printed Latin texts, and the versions.* From this period the work spread over Europe; and as it grew in popularity it expanded in size; chapters were added on such subjects as tournaments, others were enlarged, and translations into various languages were made. As I have before remarked, only one of these—the Hebrew—was taken from the Arabic, the others being made from Latin texts. These are numerous. I have myself examined thirty in the British Museum, and a little search would doubtless bring to light many more, both there and elsewhere. There are two main types, though every old copy differs from the others.

---

[1] Burton's *Anatomy of Melancholy* refers to the story, naming Porus as the king, and gives (wrongly) Q. Curtius as authority.

[2] As these stories are not told in our text, there will be no harm in summarising them here. The Queen of the South (*Nicomedia* in the early Spanish version, *India* in the Latin, *The King of India* in the Arabic and Hebrew,) fed a fair daughter on poison from the day of her birth, and sent her at maturity as a present to Alexander. Aristotle warned him of his danger, and pressed him to submit a malefactor to her embrace. As the latter died on the spot, Alexander sent her away. The other tale treats of a discussion on religion in which the Jew summarises his religious duties, and restricts his obligations to those of his own faith. The Muhammedan declares that he is bound to regard all men as brothers, whereon the Jew, who is walking, asks him to give him a ride. When the Jew is mounted he rides away, and the Muhammedan thus abandoned in the desert calls on God to assist him in the danger brought on by fulfilling his duty. Going further he comes on a lion standing beside his mule, and the rent carcase of the Jew. See the prose translation, Lamb. 501.

§ vii. *Works founded on the 'Secreta Secretorum.'*

The shorter has about sixty chapters, the longer over one hundred. Sloane 2413 is about the best MS. The printed copies, again, following the MSS. fall into two main classes. Grenville 7925 and 520 d. 5 (2), Louvain 1485. 4°. are good examples of the shorter form: 7306. a. 16 and 520. a. 12, Paris 1520. 12°. are typical of the complete book.

There are MS. commentaries on the work attributed to Bacon,[1] Scot, and other medieval writers, who all seem to have taken it quite seriously, and to have aided in spreading its fame. A copy existed some years ago at Holkham which belonged to Edward II. But a better proof of the book's popularity exists in the number of translations. Of these there are extant a very early Spanish, four Italian, and five French independent versions from the Latin. One of the latter is said to have been made in the 12th century, and so would be of special interest; but it is not yet printed.[2] I believe there are also some early German translations.

§ vii. *Works founded on the 'Secreta Secretorum.'* A work of this nature, so suitable to the habits of thought of the writers of medieval times, naturally gave rise to a host of imitations and emendations. Already in the 12th century, Giraldus Cambrensis had written a work *De Instructione Principis*, which exists in MS. in the British Museum, Cotton Julius B. XIII., an epitome of it being found in Titus. C. XII. 8. It is doubtful whether this was not an independent work in its inception: but the work of Egidio Colonna *De Regimine Principum* (a copy of which exists in Bibl. Reg. 4. D. IV. 4) is clearly based on the *Secreta Secretorum* in very great measure. Hoccleve's translation of this—his *Regement of Princes* or *De Regimine Principum*—is well known, and was edited for the Roxburghe Club in 1860.[3] Two treatises are ascribed to Innocent III. (ob. 1216), *De Administratione Principum*, and *De Eruditione Principum*: one to Thomas Aquinas, *De Regimine Principum, ad Reg. Cypri:* and one to Guill. Peraldi, *De Eruditione Principum*. Simon

---

[1] In MS. Corp. Christ. 149. Bodl. (Tanner) 116, f. 1—15.
[2] It is attributed to Petrus de Abernun, and is found in Bibl. Nat. 25407 (olim Not. Dame 5, or 277), fol. 178^b, 196. I have met with the following lines:

Primez saciez ke icest trettez *Le grant, le fiz Phelippe le rei,*
Est le secré de secrez numez, *Le fist en sa graunt vielesce*
Ke Aristotle le philosophe ydoine, *Quant de cors estreit en fieblesce,*
Le fiz Nichomache de Macedoine, *Pus qu'il ne pout pas travailler*
A sun deciple Alisandre en bone fei, *Ne al rei Alisandre repeirar.*

and Epilogue
Me ore priez, pur Deu amur, *Ke de bien fere li doint sa grace:*
En ceste fin pur le translatur *E a nus tuz issi le face,*
De cest livre, ke Pierre ad nun, *Ke le regne pussum merir,*
K'estreit est de cest de Abernun, *Ke donc a suens a sun plesir. Amen.*

[3] Dr. Furnivall's edition of it from the Harleian MS. 4866, for the E. E. T. S. is now ready for the printers.

§ viii. *The 'Secreta Secretorum.'* § ix. *The Manuscripts.* xiii

Islip, Archbishop of Canterbury (ob. 1366) wrote, while secretary to Edward III., a treatise of this nature, entitled, *Speculum Edwardi III.*: and, to mention no others, Ximenes, a Spanish bishop about 1400, wrote in Spanish, *Cresta, i.e. de Regiment de Princeps.* Such a list proves the importance of the *Secreta Secretorum* in the history of literature.[1]

§ viii. *The 'Secreta Secretorum' in English.* Our author's translation does not by any means stand alone in English; and perhaps a short description of its compeers may not be out of place. Excluding Gower's use of it in Bk. VII. of his *Confessio Amantis* and Hoccleve's (in 1412), the first separate Englishing of known date we have is the *Secreta Secretorum in English,* addressed to Jas. Butler, Earl of Ormond, Lord Deputy of Ireland, by Jas. Young, circ. 1420. It is long and rambling, omitting parts of the work, and inserting historical examples. Holmes, from whose notes much of the preceding paragraph is taken, says that the translation exists in MS. Bodl. Rawlinson 490. It will be printed for the Society with the two other prose-renderings named below.

A portion of a prose translation begun by John Shirley, in his old age, exists in the British Museum MS. 5467, f. 211. It is taken from the French, and dedicated to Henry VI. An anonymous early prose translation is in MS. 18. A. vii, in a handwriting of about 1460, written on parchment. It is a shortened Englishing of the French text of Harleian 219, and is printed, together with another anonymous prose translation from the Latin (Lambeth MS. 501), for purposes of comparison. The latter translation seems to date from the end of the 14th century, and is thus the earliest we have. Both will be printed. Warton (II. 313) describes still another, published in 4°. by Robt. and Wm. Copland in 1528, entitled, '*The Secret of Aristotyle with the Governale of Princes, and every maner of Estate,* &c.' The order of the *Sec. Sec.*, and much of its matter is made use of in *Ocia Imperialia* by Heydon, in his *Temple of Wisdom,* Lond. 1663, 8ᵛᵒ. Lastly, the *Physiognomy* is reprinted in a tract in the British Museum 519. a. 12 (3). London, 1702, 12°.

Nor is Lydgate without a rival in his poetical treatment of the *Secreta.* Sir William Forrest (Sir, because he was a clergyman) drew up and addressed to the Protector Duke of Somerset in 1548, *the Poesye of Princely Practise* for the benefit of Edward VI. The presentation copy still exists (British Museum Bibl. Reg. 17. D. III.), adorned with a drawing of Forrest presenting his work to the young king. It is well

---

[1] Thos. Rudbourne, in his Winchester History, *Angl. Sacr.* I. 242, speaking of Harold, says: 'et disciplinam Aristotelis quam dedit Alexandro sequutus fuisset,' &c., a reference to the *Sec. Sec.*

written on rather poor vellum, and extends to seventy-seven folios. It is in the same measure as our text, seven-line stanzas.

§ ix. *The Manuscripts.* A very little search convinced me that it would be of little advantage to go outside the British Museum for MSS. of the poem. Not only is there an abundance of texts there earlier than can be found elsewhere, but one of them impressed itself on me as being probably a presentation copy of the original, and as having passed under the eyes of the author of the second part, the peculiar blanks left in the text confirming the idea that the scribe intended to refer to the author. The changes of the times—the Wars of the Roses—may have prevented the work ever getting into the hands for which it was designed. I therefore determined to reproduce Sloane 2464; my reasons being, first, its early date (about 1450); second, the manifest care displayed in making the copy; third, the fullness of the text.

The facsimile which accompanies this work gives a very good idea of the writing and of the kind of ornamentation employed. It is on the same scale as the MS. itself. The rubrics are put in carefully, and the vellum is of the best quality. There is, as the MS. now stands, no trace of the original owner except a small *fleur-de-lys* stamped on the vellum. This may be the Burgundy crest, and thus may connect the book with Margaret, sister of Edward IV. The following distich is written—in a seventeenth century hand, on the last folio:

"Perusing me an ye ha doone
Conduit me home to Thos. Moone."

The other important MS. is Addit. 14,408. It is written in a northern hand, and presents some differences from Sloane 2464. I am printing some stanzas in full for the sake of comparison, and note the principal differences. It is dated 1473, and seems to represent the source of the other copies. If it had been complete, my decision in favour of Sl. 2464 would not have been so immediate; but unfortunately a page is missing, and several are injured.

HARLEIAN 4826 contains works of Lydgate and Hoccleve. ff. 52 *a* to 81 *a* contain the *Secrees*, of which unluckily one leaf is missing. It was written about 1490, on vellum, and contains some poor illuminations. As an inset it has a drawing on vellum of Lydgate presenting his 'Pilgrim' to Thos. Montacute, Earl of Salisbury—most probably a portrait.

ARUNDEL 59 contains works of Lydgate and Hoccleve. The 'Secrees' extend from fol. 90 *a* to 130 *b*, and end at stanza 352. In my judgment it was written about 1470. It is on paper, and contains a record of its

§ x. *The Text used by Lydgate.* § xi. *Summary of its History.* xv

purchase by T. Wall, Windsor Herald at Arms, at a tavern in Bishopsgate, May 8th, 1528.

HARLEIAN 2251 is Stow's copy of John Shirley's MS. It ends at the same stanza as Arundel 59, and seems to have been made from the same copy. The 'Secrees' run from 188 *b* to 224 *a*. It contains a large number of minor poems of Lydgate, and Burgh's Cato major and Cato minor (attributed to Lydgate).

LANSDOWNE 285 is of incidental interest, as having been made for the Paston family. We learn from the 'Letters' that the transcriber Ebesham was paid 1*d*. a folio for it. The volume contains also a translation of Vegetius, made for Sir Thos. Berkeley in 1408. The 'Secrees' runs from 152 *a* to 196 *b*. It was written before 1469.

SLOANE 2027 paper. 'Secrees,' 53 *a*, 92 *b*.

§ x. *The text used by Lydgate.* My next duty would naturally be to decide as to the sources from which Lydgate made his translation. I am disposed to think he either used a poor Latin text alone, or that if he used a French one, he referred to the Latin as well. The French text in Harleian 219, is the sort of copy that would have been placed at Lydgate's disposal. One feature of most of the French translations is a curious mistranslation of 'dove' for 'column' (l. 98) which arose from the substitution of *columba* for *columpna* in the Latin text—a mistake easily overlooked when a work was transcribed from dictation. Lydgate, besides falling into this mistake, follows the French translation in its omission of the story of the poison-maiden.

All argument on the subject is however vitiated by the fact that in Lydgate's work we have little more than the fragments of a translation, begun at various points, and brought together afterwards. A clear proof of this is the position of lines 974—1029, which form a part of chapter lxv in the printed text 7306 *a*. 16. It seems to me that Lydgate was struck by the lines, translated them 'to see how they looked,' and laid them by; and that after his death Burgh inserted them where they now stand. It is inconceivable that a writer of Lydgate's experience would have left ll. 638—735, and 477—602, in such a muddle as they are now in, if they were finished work; or that a veteran rhymester such as he was would have left 778 : 780 in their present state.

§ xi. *Summary of its history.* Briefly stated then, the history of our poem is this. Compiled from various sources in Syriac in the 8th century, it was translated into Arabic, with a prologue recommending Aristotle, for some Muhammedan ruler by the author. It was turned into Latin by Philip of Paris in the 13th century, thence into French, and its translation into English verse was undertaken by Lydgate, at the desire of some great personage, probably Henry VI.

§ xii. *The life of Lydgate.* Dr. Schick, in his Introduction to Lydgate's *Temple of Glas*, has devoted much care to making out a list including the known events and dates of Lydgate's life. In the first Appendix will be found a number of documents—some previously unpublished—which enable us to trace out Lydgate's history in his closing years. The grant of ten marks, Ap. 22, 1439 is particularly interesting as tending to confirm Schick's date (1430-38) against ten Brinck's (1424-33) for the *Falls of Princes*. John Baret, whose name was inserted by Lydgate's wish in the grants, was treasurer of the Abbey of St. Edmund's. His will is published by the Camden Society in their *Bury Wills*. He died in 1467. The only memorial of Lydgate he leaves is a copy of the *Story of Thebes*. Mr. Sydney Lee has been kind enough to call my attention to a ballad of Lydgate's mentioned by Bp. Alcock (b. 1430) in a sermon quoted in Brydge's *British Bibliographer*, ii. 533. This ballad, 'of which the refrain is " Englonde may wayle y^t ever Galand came here,"' was written, Alcock says, after the loss of France, Gascony, Guienne, and Normandy, *i. e.* 1452. It was published by Dr. Furnivall, *Ballads from MSS.* vol. i (Ballad Soc.), and in Hazlitt's Early English Poetry. This seems to put Lydgate's death as later than 1452. The following alterations should be made in the table, p. cxii of Dr. Schick's introduction to the *Temple of Glas*, summarising what is known of Lydgate's life and works.

1423. Lease of lands and pension granted to Lydgate and others on nomination of Rochford.
1438. Mercer's play.
1439. App. 22, grant of 10 marks yearly from the Customs of Ipswich.
1440. Easter, payment of £6 4s. 5¼d. to collector of Customs.
May 7, grant of £7 13s. 4d. yearly from proceeds of the farm of Waytelee.
Michaelmas, payment of £3 16s. 8d. to Sheriff.
1441. Nov. 14, petition for change of grant.
„ 21, patent made out to Lydgate and Baret, and the survivor of them, from the revenues of the county.
Michaelmas, payment of the year.
1443. Michaelmas, payment of £7 13s. 4d.
1446. Oct. 2, receipt of Baret for £3 16s. 8d.
1447. Epitaphium Ducis Gloucestrie.
1448. Payment of £7 13s. 4d. to Michaelmas.
1449. Payment of £7 13s. 4d. to Michaelmas.
1452. Galande Ballad.

§ xiii. *The life of Benedict Burgh.* Of Burgh, Lydgate's successor, little is known. He is usually spoken of as Magister, and his degree is attributed to Oxford without reference by Wharton. He may have been one of the Masters in Grammar who never went through the Arts course. He would be a native of the village of Burgh in Essex, though we first hear of him as rector of Sandon, and vicar of Maldon, when he was presented to the former living, July 6th, 1440, by Thomas, seventh Baron de Scales. At this time he held the position of tutor to William, son of Henry Bourchier, afterwards Earl of Essex, who had married Isabel, daughter of Richard Earl of Cambridge, sister of Richard Duke of York, and aunt to Edward IV. Burgh thus became acquainted with the York family, and another of his pupils, Henry Bourchier, married the daughter of the Lord Scales, who gave Burgh the living of Sandon.[1]

In Add. 29729, fol. 6 *a*, we find a short poem written by Benedict Burgh to Lydgate. It is most unfortunate that the top of it has been cut down in binding, as it would seem to have given some information connecting Lydgate with Windsor, from which we could have fixed a date. It appears to be the means by which Burgh introduced himself to the notice of the famous old writer. At this time he entertained hopes of becoming acquainted with Lydgate, and of obtaining help from him in his studies. I have added this in an Appendix [2]. We may imagine that Lydgate lent him his friendly aid and guiding criticism; and under these auspices Burgh produced the translation of Cato's Distiches,[2] printed by Caxton about 1478, and alluded to by him in his Forewords to his own translation. Beleigh Abbey is a mile from Maldon, and Bourchier was buried there.

Burgh resigned his living of Sandon in Sept. 1444,[3] and does not seem to have held any other preferment till Oct. 19, 1450, when he became rector of Hedingham Sibele, a Bourchier living in the same county. Much of this interval he spent, doubtless in company with Lydgate, and soon after his death, Burgh was called upon to complete our poem—to act as the Monk of Bury's literary executor, in fact—either by Viscount Bourchier, or even by the king himself, with whom Lydgate seems to have been a favourite. Probably the living was Burgh's

---

[1] I am indebted to the Rev. B. Wright, Rector of Sandon, for a copy of some entries, proving rather curiously that Burgh's predecessor was Vicar of All Saints, Maldon.

[2] Lond. (about) 1478. 4°. (Camb. A. B 8. 48. [2 editions]), London 1558. 8°. (Mus. Brit. G. 9792).

[3] His successor entered on his duties Sep. 24, 1444.

xviii   § xiv. *Remarks on the Poem.*   § xv. *The Metre of the Poem.*

reward. Through the same influence he was appointed Archdeacon of Colchester, Feb. 10, 1465, and on Feb. 23, 1472, a prebendary of St. Paul's, his former pupil being now brother-in-law of Edward IV. In Feb. 1476, he was made a Canon of St. Stephen's at Westminster, and thereon resigned his living and prebend. This post of honour and dignity he held till his death, July 13th, 1483, the same year as witnessed the decease of his old patron, Henry Bourchier. It was while Canon of St. Stephen's that Burgh made Caxton's acquaintance, and got his translation published. Burgh's name is preserved among the benefactors of St. Stephen's (Cott. Faustina, B. viii. [1, 2]), and his benefaction must have been of some value, since the grants to the clergy present at his anniversary mass are on a fairly liberal scale.

Other works of Burgh's are, *A Christmas Game*, in *Christmas Carols*, ed. 1841 by Wright for the *Percy Society*, and in *Notes and Queries*, May 16, 1868, by Dr. Furnivall; *Aristotle's A B C*, in the *Babees Book*, edited by Dr. Furnivall for the *E. E. T. S.* 1868, and a balade in Add. 29729, following that given in our Appendix. Some of the shorter pieces attributed to Lydgate may also have been written by Burgh.

§ xiv. *Remarks on the poem.* Considered as literature, the work before us is empty of interest. It would in any case have been difficult to make poetry out of the *Secreta Secretorum*, and only in one stanza does Lydgate come near it. His work is scrappy, ill-ordered, and tedious to a remarkable degree even for him. Nor has it much bearing on the science of his time. Doubtless, if Lydgate had lived, he would have revised his work, but precisely because of his death, and the piety of his 'young follower,' who did not allow himself to alter the last writings of his dead master, we see the seven-line stanza in the making. This seems to me to be the main point of interest to us in it. Burgh's work appears to me to affect a more archaic tone than Lydgate's; of his stanzas, the prolog seems the best,—it has been printed by Halliwell in the preface to his collection of Lydgate's shorter poems. Lines 477—602 and 974—1029 were printed by Ashmole in his *Theatrum Chemicum Britannicum*, London 1652, 4°.

§ xv. *The metre of the poem.* The work is written in Rhyme Royal, in seven-line stanzas of ten-syllable lines with rhymes $a\,b\,a\,b\,b\,c\,c$. Dr. Schick, whose Introduction to the *Temple of Glas* is indispensable to every reader of Lydgate, enumerates five varieties of verse. Students should however be warned that its prosody is the weak point of Dr. Schick's work.

§ xvi. *The Rhyme.*

A. Five iambics, with sometimes an extra syllable at the end, and usually a well-defined cæsura after the second foot:
  l. 9. The lórd to plése / and hís lawés to képe.
B. Lines with an extra syllable before the cæsura:
  l. 33. For prúdent prínces / most dígne of Réverénce.
C. The peculiar Lydgatian type in which the two accented syllables clash: l. 167. Whan thís is dóon / férthermóre in déde
D. The headless line, in which the first syllable is cut off:
  l. 135. Moóst notáble / and dígne of Réuerénce.
E. Lines with trisyllabic first measure:
  l. 171. Coúnt ŏf thĕr Cítees / the fámous Góvernáunce.

To these I would add, that some of Lydgate's lines scan only on the assumption that they are six-measure lines:
  l. 1365. Ánd thĕ trănslácyŏun ŏf Thómăs / mártryd ĭn Crýstĕmásse.
  l. 1496. Thĕ dúlnĕsse óf my pénne / yŏw bĕséchyng ténlŭmýne.

Line 1497 may be best scanned on this assumption; but, as Schick remarks, many of Lydgate's lines scan in several different ways. I suggest, with all due deference, that as Lydgate broke nearly every rule of the Rhyme Royal, there is no reason for supposing that he kept to a five-beat measure. In fact, the greater part of the *Secrees* could be scanned on a six-beat basis with little trouble by allowing a liberal use of the pause.

Assuming that a ten-syllable verse is the normal one, I have scanned the whole of the poem, and counting no slurred syllables, I get the following results:

Lydgate in 1491 lines has
  1   14-syllable line
  2   13-syllable lines
  46 12   „   „
  223 11   „   „
  287 9   „   „
  40   8   „   „
  2   7   „   „
  ___
  601

Burgh in 1239 lines has
  1   14-syllable line
  5   13-syllable lines
  71 12   „   „
  217 11   „   „
  235 9   „   „
  84   8   „   „
  4   7   „   „
  ___
  617

§ xvi. *The Rhyme.* I must again refer the reader to Dr. Schick for general principles, noting here only points of special prominence in the poem. The rhyme is very good in Lydgate, and fairly good in Burgh. There is a marked assonance in l. 8 kepe : slepe : meke. l. 778, grucchyng is made to rhyme with itself; l. 1003 kynde : Ynde : kynde; l. 1164 degre : mutabilite : degre; l. 1069 shrewys : the wys; l. 1072 xx § xvii. *General Characteristics of Lydgate's Language.*

cherche : werche ; l. 281 desirs : cleer is. Stanza 176 is altogether in a muddle, the rhymes being *a b a a a c c*.

Many of the rhymes are cheap : l. 50 corage : age : outrage ; l. 286 Eyer : Repayer ; l. 615 tarye : solitarye ; l. 1112 partye : Jupartye ; l. 1419 accorde : O corde. Before concluding that Lydgate's rhymes are impure, we must bear in mind our own double pronunciation of such words as *wind* and *wan*, to suit the rhyme.

Turning to Burgh, we note in his rhyme much greater weakness. Such rhymes as l. 1527 tryvyal : equal; l. 1597 fat : estat; l. 1604 parfightly : body ; l. 1702 egir : wedir ; l. 1952 mesurably : body ; l. 2008 specially : remedy ; l. 2150 trewly : contrary : feithfully ; l. 2651 angry : fooly ; are hardly ever met in Lydgate. l. 1602 tyme : ffyne ; l. 1882 began : nigram ; l. 1987 venym : wyn ; l. 2136 Oon : boorn ; l. 2171 man : can : wysdam ; l. 2668 knee : slevys ; are examples of another fault uncommon in the Monk of Bury. Burgh is also markedly careless of his vowels in the rhyme. l. 2360 mynde : sende : condiscende ; and l. 2304 Rebeel : feel : Cel ; cannot ever have rhymed.

§ xvii. *General characteristics of Lydgate's language.* The most striking feature of the language is that it is so modern. The final *e* is rarely sounded in words of Old English origin, and still more rarely in those of French. The influence of the fifty years since Chaucer shows itself in this work, which should be compared with one of Lydgate's earlier poems in this respect. The plural is, more often than not, sounded as our own is, *i. e.* not sounded at all as a separate syllable, and the plural of adjectives is dropped, the *e* in *hih* seems to be plural (ll. 440, 715), but not uniformly so. French nouns are generally sounded with *e* mute (e̥), as l. 398 rwyne̥, l. 402 shadwe̥, owmbre̥, l. 656 folwe̥, l. 1309 salwe̥, l. 1611 malwe̥, l. 1807 morwe̥. The *e* in composition is not invariably sounded as mode̥ffye, l. 1204. I had prepared some notes on the accidence of Lydgate, but the appearance of *The Temple of Glas* has rendered it unnecessary, and I accordingly reserve any remarks for the notes.

The mannerisms of Lydgate are well to the fore here. His modesty —'the Rudnesse of my style,' l. 21 ;—the phrases he repeats to fill up a line—' this to seyn,' ' set in ordre,' ' it is also of hym maad mencioun,' ' by Recoord of scripture,' ' in especial,' ' lyk our entencyouns,' ' In sentence breef,' ' for short conclusyoun ' ;—and the familiar metaphor ' I have no Colour, but Oonly Chalk and sable.' Burgh has well imitated his master's envoy—if indeed Lydgate did not write it himself; it recalls some of his earlier ones in several respects.

A recent editor of Lydgate has spoken of the 'Philistine maxims' of the Secrees. I am afraid that some of us, who live on the borderland, and are often driven by the bumptiousness of the chosen people to serve a campaign under the banners of Philistia, are not the best judges on the matter. Still, it has been a pleasure to me to add to the notes such scraps of a discursive reading as will tend to show that the maxims of the *Secreta Secretorum* were the commonplaces of such Philistines as Cicero and Plutarch,—of all classical antiquity. In the case of such a work one can hope no more, nor indeed is more required.

I have to express my gratitude to the authorities and attendants of the Manuscript Room at the British Museum for their kindness and courtesy, and to acknowledge with gratitude the debt I owe—in common, I believe, with every one who seeks his advice and help—to the Director of the Society, Dr. Furnivall.

Modern School, Bedford, July 1892.

APPENDIX I.

DOCUMENTS RELATING TO LYDGATE.

I. The dates of Lydgate's orders are given in Cotton. Tib. B. IX. f. 35ᵇ. 69ᵇ. 85ᵇ.

Subdeacon, 17th (Nov. ?), 1389.
Deacon, 28th May, 1393.
Priest, 4th April, 1397.

II. Lease to Dan John Lydgate and others by Sir Ralph Rochford of the lands of the alien Priory of Longville Gifford, or Newenton Longville, with the pension of Spalding, formerly appertaining to the Abbey of Angers, by virtue of letters patent of Henry IV. and Henry V. to the said Sir Ralph Rochford.

Nicolas's Acts of the Privy Council, III. 40.

(MS. Cotton. Cleopatra, F. IV. f. 7.)

xxj° die Februarij anno primo apud Westmonasterium, presentibus dominis Ducibus Gloucestrie et Exonie, Archiepiscopo Cantuariensi, Londoniensi Wyntoniensi et Wygorniensi Episcopis, Marchie Warrewici et Northumbrie Comitibus, Cromwell' Tiptoft et Hungerford',[1] Cancellario Thesaurario et Custode privati sigilli, concessum erat quod omnia terre et tenementa pertinencia prioratui Sancte Fidis de Longville (alienigene alias dicto prioratui de Longville Gifford, alias dicto prioratui de Newenton' Longville) cum pertinenciis in regno Anglie una cum omnibus aliis maneriis terris pratis redditibus, boscis, molendinis, porcionibus, pensionibus, feodis, rectoriis, reversionibus, juribus, communis, dominiis, exitibus, emolumentis, revencionibus, et hereditacionibus quibuscumque, et pensione de Spaldyng valoris xl. li. per annum abbathie de Aungiers, dudum pertinentibus secundum formam et effecium literarum patencium dominorum Henrici quarti et

A.D. 1423, Feb. 21.

Present the Privy Council,

it was allowed that the lands and rents of the Alien Priory,

with the pension of £40 per annum of the Abbey of Angers,

[1] Dominis omitted?

Appx. I.—*Lease and Grant to Lydgate*, 1423-40.

should go to Dan John Lydgate and three others,

on the nomination of Sir Ralph Rocheford,

Henrici quinti Regum Anglie Radulpho Rocheford' militi inde concessarum et confirmatarum dimittantur, modo ad firmam Dompno Iohanni Lidgate et Iohanni de Tofte monachis, Iohanni Glaston' et Willelmo Malton' capellanis ad nominacionem prefati Radulphi Rocheford' sine aliquo inde reddendo, quousque dicto Radulpho provisum fuerit de recompensa conveniente ad terminum vite sue ad valorem annuum terrarum et tenementorum predictorum, prout sibi promissum fuit per dominum Regem defunctum patrem Regis nunc apud Dovorr'.

given at Dover.

III. A grant of 10 marks to Lydgate from the Customs at Ipswich.

Patent Roll, 17 Henry VI., p. 1, m. 7.

Pro Johanne Lydgate Monacho.

1439, April 22.

10 marks

from the customs

of Ipswich,

to be paid at Michaelmas and Easter in equal portions.

Rex Omnibus ad quos etc. salutem. Sciatis quod de gracia nostra speciali, ac pro bono et gratuito seruicio quod dilectus nobis Johannes Lydgate, Monachus Monasterij siue Abbathie de Bury Sancti Edmundi, tam Carissimo Domino et Patri nostro ac Auunculis nostris defunctis quam nobis et carissimo Auunculo nostro Humfrido Duci Gloucestrie adhuc superstiti ante hec tempora multipliciter impendit, concessimus eidem Johanni decem marcas percipiendas annuatim, pro termino vite sue, tam de antiqua et parua custumis nostris, quam de subsidio lanarum coriorum et pellium lanutarum, necnon de subsidio trium solidorum de dolio et duodecim denariorum de libra, in portu ville Gippewici per manus Custumariorum siue Collectorum custumarum et subsidiorum predictorum in portu predicto pro tempore existencium, ad terminos Sancti Michaelis et Pasche, per equales porciones. In cuius etc. Teste Rege apud Castrum suum de Wyndesore, xxij die Aprilis.

per breue de priuato sigillo.

IV. Allowance of payment of this Grant, £6 4s. 5¼d. being the proportion due at Easter 1440.

Enrolled Accounts, Exchequer (Lord Treasurer's Remembrancer), Customs, No. 20.

Account of Walter Green and Thomas West, Collectors of Customs and Subsidies in the Port of Ipswich from Michaelmas, 18 Henry VI. to Michaelmas 19 Henry VI. Among the payments is the following:

Appx. I.—*A Payment; and a Grant of* 10 *Marks a year,* 1440.   xxv

Et Joh*anni* Lyddegate Monacho Monaste*r*ij siue Abb*ath*ie de Bury S*an*c*t*i Ed*mundi*, cui Rex xxij^{do}. die A'prilis, Anno decimo septimo, concessit decem marcas percipiend*as* annuatim p*ro* te*r*mi*no* vite sue tam de antiqua *et* p*ar*ua custumis Regis, q*uam* de subsidio lana*rum* corio*rum* et pelli*um* lan*u*ta*rum*, necnon de subs*idio* tri*um* solido*rum* de dolio *et* duodecim denario*rum* de libra, in portu ville Gippewic*i* p*er* manus Custumario*rum* siue Collecto*rum* custuma*rum* et subsidio*rum* p*re*dicto*rum* in portu p*re*di*c*to p*ro* temp*or*e existenc*ium*, ad te*r*minos S*an*cti Michaelis et Pasche per equales porcio*nes*. vide*l*icet de hui*usmod*i .x. marc*is* pe*r* annu*m* a p*re*di*c*to .xx^{mo} ij^{do}. die Aprilis di*c*to Anno .xvij^{mo}.—vsq*ue* festu*m* Pasche p*ro*ximo sequentem Anno .xviij^{uo}. vj. li. iiij. s. v. d. q^a. per br*eu*e Regis ir*r*ot*ul*at*um* in Memorand*is* de anno .xix^{no}. Regis huius te*r*mino Sa*n*cti Hillar*ij*. Rot*u*lo .x^{mo}. *et* li*t*eras patentes ipsius Johannis de rec*i*pcione.

To Jn. Lydgate (under the Grant of 22 April 1439)

10 marks a year, on part of his Annuity namely £6 4s. 5¼d. to Easter 1440.

V. The King cancels the previous grant of A.D. 1439 of 10 marks, and grants to Lydgate £7 13s. 4d. per annum from the proceeds of the farm of Waytefee, to date from the Easter preceding.

Patent Roll, 18 Henry VI., p. 2, m. 5.

Pro Johanne Lydgate Monacho.

Rex Omn*ibus* ad quos etc. / sal*u*tem. Sciatis quod cum Joh*ann*es Lydgate Monachus de Bury S*an*c*t*i Edmundi ha*b*ens ex concessione nos*t*ra decem marcas percipiend*as* annuatim durante vita sua de custumis de Ippeswych' per manus Custumario*rum* ibidem p*ro* tempore existenc*ium* prout in l*ite*ris nostris patentib*us* inde confec*t*is plenius apparet in voluntate existat easdem l*i*teras in Cancell*ari*a*m* nos*t*ram restituere cancelland*as* ad effec*tum* quod nos eidem Johanni septem libras tresdecim solidos et quatu*or* denarios percipiend*os* annuatim p*ro* termino vite sue de exitib*us* et proficuis de alba firma *et* feodo vulgariter nuncupato Waytefee, in Com*itatibus* Norffolcie et Suffo*l*c*i*e, concedere dignare*mur*. Nos, de gr*ac*ia nos*t*ra speciali, ac pro eo q*uo*d idem Joh*ann*es d*i*ctas l*i*teras nos*t*ras in Cancell*ari*a*m* nos*t*ram restituit cancelland*as*, concessim*us* eidem Johanni d*i*ctos septem libras tresdecim solidos et quatuor denarios percipiend*os* annuatim, durante vita sua, a festo Pasche vltimo p*re*terito, de exitib*us*

1440, May 7.

£6 13s. 4d. a year for life

to be canseld for £7 13s. 4d. a year for life.

£7 13s. 4d.

Appx. I.—*Payment to Lydgate*, 1440. *His Petition.*

through the Abbot of Bury St. Edmunds.

et proficuis provenientibus de alba firma et feodo vulgariter nuncupato Waytefee predicto, per manus Abbatis de Bury Sancti Edmundi pro tempore existentis, et sic deinceps ad terminos Sancti Michaelis et Pasche per equales porciones durante vita sua predicta. In cuius etc. Teste Rege, apud Westmonasterium

Extractum.[1] vij die Maij.

per ipsum Regem.

VI. An allowance to the Sheriff of £3 16s. 8d., paid to Lydgate (and Baret) on account of the grant, no. VIII.

Pipe Roll, 19 Henry VI. Norfolk and Suffolk.

Adhuc Item Norff'.

For the year * 18 Hen. VI. 1439-40.

Milo Stapilton' nuper Vicecomes de anno precedenti* debet CCClxxix. li. xj. s. vij. d. ob. qª.

[Among his allowances is the following:]

the grant of Nov. 21, 1441, is quoted.

The grant due from Easter 1440

of £3 16s. 8d. was paid for Mich. 19 Hen. VI. 1440.

Et Johanni Lidgate, Monacho de Bury Sancti Edmundi, et Johanni Baret Armigero, quibus Rex xxjᵐᵒ die Nouembris anno xxᵐᵒ concessit septem libras tresdecim solidos et quatuor denarios percipiendos annuatim a festo Pasche anno xviijᵘᵒ durante vita sua et alterius eorum diucius viuentis de exitibus proficuis firmis et reuencionibus Comitatuum Norff' et Suff' prouenientibus per manus Vicecomitis eorundem Comitatuum pro tempore existentis ad festa Pasche et Sancti Michaelis per equales porciones— lxxvj. s. viij. d. de termino Sancti Michaelis anno xixⁿᵒ. per breue Regis irrotulatum in Memorandis de anno xxᵐᵒ Regis huius. termino Sancti Michaelis. rotulo .xxxiiijᵗᵒ. et literas patentes ipsorum Iohannis et Iohannis de recepcione.

VII. Petition of John Lydgate, monk of Bury, touching the invalidity of letters patent granting him £7 13s. 4d. yearly, and praying new letters patent to him and John Baret, squire. Granted.

Acts of the Privy Council, V. 156. (20 Hen. VI.)

MS. Addit. 4609, art. 27. Lydgate's Petition to the King, with the Answer.

[1] This means that an extract of this grant was sent to the Exchequer: it will probably be found in the Originalia Rolls.

Appx. I.—*Lydgate's Petition for a Grant to him and Baret.* xxvii

Unto the King oure most gratious soveraign lord.

Besechith you mekely youre pouere and perpetuell oratour John Lydgate, monke of Bury Seint Edmond. For as moche as for diverses opinions had in lawe be your justices and barons of youre eschequer, youre le*tt*res patentes grauntid to youre seid besecher of vij. li. xiij. s. iiij. d. may not take effecte to the wele and profite of youre seid besecher.

That it may please unto youre hyenesse to grante unto your seid besecher and to John Baret squier, youre graciouses letters patentes undir youre grete seal, after the fourme contenue and effecte of a cedule to this bille annexid, and there-vpon youre liberate currant and allocate dormant in due fourme, for the whiche youre seid besecher shall restore youre gratiouses letters patentes to him made of vij. li. xiij. s. iiij. d. to be taken be the handes of the Abbot of Bury into the chauncerye to be cancellid. And he shall pray to God for you.

Rex apud West*monasterium* xiiij° die Novembr*is* anno xx. concessit præsentem billam ut petitur, et mandavit Custodi privati sigilli sui facere garrantu*m* Cancellario Angl*ie*, ut ipse desuper fieri faci*at* litteras paten*tes* secundum tenorem copie presentibus annexe, presen*tibus* Dom*i*no Suff*olcie* qui billam prosecutus est ac me,

Adam Moleyns.

1441, Nov. 14.

£7 13s. 4d.

The King grants the petition,

present the Earl of Suffolk.

VIII. The King's patent granting to Lydgate and Baret, and to the survivor, the sum of £7 13s. 4d. per annum.

Patent Roll, 20 Henry VI., p. 1, m. 20.

P*ro* Johan*n*e Lidgate Monacho et Johan*n*e Baret Armige*ro*.

Rex Om*n*ibus ad quos etc. sal*u*tem. Sciatis q*uod* cum nos septimo die Maij, Anno regni n*ost*ri decimo octauo, concesserim*us* Johan*n*i Lidgate, Monacho de Bury Sa*n*c*t*i Edmundi, septem libras tresdecim solidos *et* quatuor denarios, percipie*n*d*os* annuatim a festo Pasche tunc vltimo prete*r*ito, durante vita sua, de exit*ibus* et proficuis p*ro*uenie*n*tib*us* de alba firma *et* feodo vulgariter nuncupato Waytefe, p*er* manus Abbatis de Bury Sa*n*cti Edmundi p*ro* tempore existe*n*t*is*, et sic deinceps ad te*r*minos Sa*n*cti Mich*ae*lis et Pasche p*er* equales porc*i*ones p*ro*ut in l*i*teris

1441, Nov. 21.

Lydgate's Annuity of £7 13s. 4d.

Appx. I.—*Grant of Pension to Lydgate and Baret*, A.D. 1441.

nostris patentibus inde sibi confectis plenius continetur. Et quia idem Johannes in voluntate existit dictas literas nostras in Cancellariam nostram ibidem restituendi cancellandas, ad intencionem quod nos sibi ac Johanni Baret Armigero septem libras tresdecim solidos et quatuor denarios percipiendos annuatim durante vita sua et alterius eorum diucius viuentis de exitibus proficuis firmis et reuencionibus Comitatuum Norffolcie et Suffolcie concedere dignaremur; Nos premissa considerantes, ac bona et gratuita seruicia que dicti Johannes et Johannes nobis impenderunt et impendent infuturum, ac pro eo quod idem Johannes Lidgate literas predictas nobis in Cancellariam predictam restituit cancellandas, de gracia nostra speciali concessimus eisdem Johanni et Johanni, septem libras tresdecim solidos et quatuor denarios percipiendos annuatim a dicto festo Pasche durante vita sua et alterius eorum diucius viuentis, de exitibus proficuis firmis et reuencionibus Comitatuum predictorum per manus Vicecomitis eorundem Comitatuum pro tempore existentis, ad festa Pasche et Sancti Michaelis per equales porciones. In cuius etc. *Teste Rege apud* Westmonasterium, xxj die Nouembris.

Per breue de priuato sigillo, et de data predicta, auctoritate Parliamenti.

to be cansold for a like Annuity to him and Jn. Baret.

IX. Payment to Michaelmas 1441.
Pipe Roll, 22 Henry VI. (1443-4)

Norfolk and Suffolk.

Roger Chamberleyn, late Sheriff of the 19th year, renders account of 7*l*. 13*s*. 4*d*. paid to John Lidgate & John Baret, as above, for the term of Easter 19 Henry VI. and the term of Michaelmas 20 Henry VI. [1441], by writ enrolled in the Memoranda of Trinity 20 Henry VI., roll 13, and their letters of acquittance.

[The writ referred to is extant in the Exchequer Memoranda Roll, on the side of the King's Remembrancer.]

£7 13s. 4d. to Michaelmas 1441.

X. Payment to Michaelmas 1443.
Pipe Roll, 21 Henry VI. (1442-3).

Norfolk and Suffolk.

Thomas Brewes, Sheriff (for this year), paid to John Lidgate and John Baret, as before, 7*l*. 13*s*. 4*d*. for the term of Easter 21

£7 13s. 4d. to

Appx. I.—*Payments to Lydgate and Baret,* 1443-6.   xxix

Henry VI. and the term of Michaelmas 22 Henry VI. [1443], by the King's writ among the *Communia* of Trinity term 21 Henry VI., roll 5, and by the letters of acquittance of "the same John." *Michaelmas 1443.*

[The Writ referred to is extant in the Exchequer Memoranda Roll, on the side of the King's Remembrancer. It orders the Sheriff for the time being to pay the annuity from time to time, without further warrant, as the King would be satisfied with an acquittance on each occasion.]

XI. Receipt of Baret, 2nd October, 1446, published by Zupitza, *Anglia,* III. 532.

Nouer*i*nt vniu*er*si p*er* presentes me Joha*nn*em Baret armigerum recepisse p*r*o me *et* Joha*nn*e Lydgate Monacho de Bury s*an*c*t*i Edm*u*ndi, de Wille*l*m*o* Tyrell, Vicecomite Norffolcie *et* Suffolcie, tres libras, sexdecim solidos, *et* quatuor [octo?] denarios, de illis septem libris, tresdecim solidis, *et* quatuor denariis quos Dom*i*nus Rex p*er l*itt*er*as suas patentes nob*is* concessit percipiendo*s* a*n*nuati*m* ad terminum vite no*s*tre *et* alterius nostru*m* diuicius viuentis, de exitibus, p*r*oficuis, ffirmis, *et* reuenc*i*onib*us* Com*ita*tuu*m* p*r*edicto*r*um p*er* manu*s* Vicecom*i*tis eorundem, qui p*r*o tempore fue*r*it, ad festa Pasche et s*an*c*t*i Mich*a*e*l*is per equales porc*i*ones, videl*i*cet p*r*o term*in*o Mich*a*e*l*is vltimo preterito ante data*m* presenciu*m*. De quib*us* vero tribu*s* libris sexdecim solidis *et* octo denariis, p*r*o termino Mich*a*e*l*is predi*c*to, fateor me p*r*o me *et* predi*c*to Joha*n*ne Lydgate esse pacatu*m*, dictu*m*que vicecomi*·*tem inde fore quietu*m* p*er* presentes. In cui*us* rei testimoniu*m* presentib*us* sigillu*m* meu*m* apposui. Datu*m* secundo die Octobr*is* anno regni Regis Henrici sexto post conquestum vicesimo quinto.

John Baret receives from Wm. Tyrell, Sheriff of Norfolk (24 H. VI.),

£3 16s. 8d. on account of himself and Lydgate,

Oct. 2, 1446.

[This payment by Sheriff William Tyrell has not been found in the Pipe Rolls, though sundry portions of his accounts are recorded from the 26th to the 33rd year of the reign. The rolls have been searched down to 2 Edw. IV., but only two later entries have been discovered, as below.]

Appx. I.—*Payments to Lydgate and Baret*, 1448-49. Appx. II.

XII. Payment to Michaelmas 1448.

Pipe Roll, 32 Henry VI. Res. Norf., dorse.

Philip Wentworth, late Sheriff of the 26th. year, renders a further account, showing the payment to John Lidegate, monk of Bury St. Edmund's, and John Baret, Esquire, of 7^l. 13^s. 4^d., under the King's grant of 21 November 20 Henry VI., for the terms of Easter in the 26th. year and Michaelmas in the 27th year, by the King's writ in Trinity term in the 21st. year, and by letters of acquittance of " the same John."

XIII. Payment to Michaelmas 1449.

Pipe Roll, 32 Henry VI. Adhuc Item Norf., dorse.

Giles Seintlo, Esquire, late Sheriff of the 27th. year, renders a further account, showing the payment to John Lidegate, monk of Bury St. Edmund's, and John Baret, Esquire, of 7^l. 13^s. 4^d. for the terms of Easter in the 27th. year and Michaelmas in the 28th. year, by writ of Trinity term in the 21st. year, and the letters of acquittance of " the same John."

APPENDIX II.

THE IX PROPERTIES OF WYNE

per Iohnen Lidgate.

Additional MS. 29729, f. 16ª, Brit. Mus.

Wyne of nature hathe properties nyne:
Comfortythe coragis; clarifiethe the syght;
Gladdeth the herte, this lycor most devyne;
Hetythe the stomake, of his natural myght;
Sharpithe wittis; gevith hardines in fight;
Clensyth wounds; engendrithe gentyll blode.
Licor of licor, at festis makyth men lyght,
Scoureth ye palat, through fyne ye color good.

APPENDIX III. (B. M. Addit. MS. 29729.)

A POEM IN PRAISE OF LIDGATE,
WRITTEN BY BENEDICT BURGH BEFORE THEY WERE ACQUAINTED.

[Written by] Mas^{r.} Burgh in þe prays of Iohn Lidgate * * * *
booke dwelyng at wyndsor.

(1)

Nat dremyd I in ye mount of pernaso,   1   [fol. 6 a]
   ne dranke I nevar at pegases welle,   Burgh does
the pale pirus saw I never also   not begin in
   ne wist I nevar where ye muses dwelle,   the usual style.
Ne of goldyn tagus can I no thynge telle;   5
    And to wete my lippis I cowde not atteyne
      In Cicero, or Elicon sustres tweyne.   7

(2)

   The crafte of speche that some tyme formde w[e]s [was in MS.]   8   He has not the craft of
    Of the famous philosophers [m]oste perfite,   n in MS.   speech of
Aristotell, Gorge, and ermogenes,   Aristotle,
   Nat have I, so I have lerid but a lite;   Gorgias, and Hermogenes,
    As for my party, thowgh I repent, I may go qwite.   12
     Of tullius, frauncis, & quintilian   Cicero,
      fayne wolde I lere, but I not conceyve can.   14   Petrarch, and Quintilian.

(3)

The noble poete virgile the mantuan,   15   He enumer-
   Omere the greke, and torqwat sovereyne,   ates the poets beaten by
Naso also that sith this worlde firste be-gan   Lydgate from Homer
   the marvelist transformynge all best can devyne,
   Terence ye mery and pleasant theatryne,   19
    Porcyus, lucan, marycan, and orace,
     Stace, Juvenall, and the lauriate bocase,   21   to Boccacio.

(4)

All thes hathe peyne, youre Innate sapience,   22   While Lydgate lives
   Ye have gadred flouris in this motli mede,
to yow is yeven the verray price of excellence,
   thowghe they be go yet the wordis be not dede;   Poesy is not dead.
    thenlumynyd boke where in a man shall rede   26
PHILOSOPHERS.

Appx. III.—*Burgh's Praise of Lydgate.*

thes & mo, be in this londe legeble,
Ye be the same, ye¹ be the goldyn bible. [¹ *ye in MS.*]   28

(5)

O yet I truste to be holde & see   29
  this blisful booke with yᵉ golden clasppes seven,
ther I wyll begyne and lerne myne a. b. c. ;
that were my paradyse, that wer my heuen,
gretar filicitie can no man neven,   33
so god my sowle save 'di benedicite.'
Maister lidgate, what man be ye ?   35

(6)

Now God, my maister, preserve yow longe on lyve,   36
  that yet I may be your prentice or I dye,
then sholde myne herte at ye porte of blise aryve ;
ye be the flowre and tresure of poise,
the garland of Ive, and laure of victorye.   40
  by my trowghte, & I myght ben a emperour,
for your konynge I shulde your heres honor.   42

(7)

Writen at thabbey of bylegh, chebri place,   43
  With frosti fingers, and nothynge pliaunt,
when from the high hille, I men ye mount Canace,
was sent in to briton the stormy persaunt
that made me loke as lede, & chaunge semblaunt,   47
And eke ye sturdi wynde of Yperborye,
Made me of chere, vnlusti sadde & sory.   49

(8)

The laste moneth that men clepe decembre,   50
  When phebus share was driven a boute yᵉ heven,
yf we reken a ryght & well remembre,
four tymes onys, & aftar ward seven,
that is to sey passid ther was days aleven   54
Of the moneth when this vnadvisid lettar
writ was, but with your helpe here aftar bettar.   56

Marginal notes:
- *Burgh hopes to see and hear him.*
- [fol. 6 b.] *He wishes to be his prentice.*
- *The poem written at Bylegh Abbey in a cold north wind.*
- *December 11th, 144—.*

l. 10. This Hermogenes is the rhetorician (*see* Quintilian).
l. 17. Torqwat : can this be *Boethius* (*A. M. Torquatus Severinus*), or is it a word for *crowned?*
l. 20. Porcius is Cato (distiches), Marycan is Capella.
l. 21. Stace, Statius.

APPENDIX IV.

SPECIMENS OF ADDIT. MS. 14408, BRIT. MUS.
Stanzas 140-3 and 328-31.

Howe Aristotylle declarith to kyng Alisaundre of þe stonys.

(140)

Towchyng þe stone of philosofris olde,   974
  Of weche thay make most soverayn mencyon,
But there is oon, as aristotylle tolde,
  Which alle excellith in comperison,
  Stone of stones, most soverayne of renowne;   978
    towchyng þe vertu of this ryche thyng
    thus he wrote to þe most soverayne kyng.   980

(141)

O alisaundre, grettist of dignite,   981
  And of þe worlde monarke and regent,
And of alle nacions hast the sovereynte,
  Eche oon to obeye and be obedient;
  And to conclude the fyne of oure entent,   985
    Alle worldely tresoure breeflie schete in oon,
    is declared in vertue of this stone.   987

(142)

Thow muste fyrste conceyve in substaunce,   988
  by a maner vnkouth diuision,
Water frome eyre make a disseueraunce,
  And fyre frome eyre by a deperticion;
  Eche one preseruid from corrupcion,   992
    As philosofirs aforne haue specified,
    Which by reason may not be denyed.   994

(143)

Watere frome eyre departed prudentlie,   995
  Eyre frome fyre, and fyre from erthe doon,

Appx. IV.—*Sample of Addit. MS. 14,408, Brit. Mus.*

 the crafte conceyued, deuydyd trewlie,
  Withouten erroure or decepcion,
  Put every element in his compleccion,   999
   As it apertenyth to his parte,
   As is remembrid perfitlie in this arte.   1001
.·. . . . .

(328)
It is to be titelyd how prevyd withoute obstacle,   2290
 As oolde philosofris put in remembraunce,
þat in man is founde grete myracle,
 namyd þe lytulle worlde by autores allegaunce;
 ffor many vnkouthe and dyuerse circumstaunce   2294
  founde in hym, moste soverayne creature,
  namyd beste resonable by intelligence in sure.   2296

(329)
He is hardy as a lyon, dredfulle as þe hare,   2297
 large as þe cok, and as a hound couetous,
harde as a herte in forest which doth fare;
 Buxum as þe tyrtylle, as lionesse dispitous,
 Simple as þe lambe, lyke þe foxe malicious,   2301
  Swyfte as the Roo, as bere slowe in taryeng,
  and lyke þe Elefaunt precious in ech thyng.   2303

(330)
As þe asse vile and contagious,   2304
 and a lytelle kyng hasty and rebelle;
Chaste as aungelle, as swyne lecherous,
 Meke as þe pecock, and as a bole wode and feel;
 Profitable as þe bee in his hyve which is selle,   2308
  ffayre as þe horse, as þe owle malicious,
  dombe as þe fische, and as a mouse noyous.   2310

(331)
Note this processe in þe audith countable,   2311
 Of þe remembraunce, and knowe redelie
þat in beeste nor thyng vegetable
 No thyng may be vniuersally,
 But if it be founde naturally   2315
  In mannes nature; wherfor of oon accorde
  Olde philesofris callidy hym þe lytelle worlde.   2317

LYDGATE AND BURGH'S[1] "SECREES OF OLD PHILISOFFRES."

[*Sloane MS.* 2464, *British Museum.*]

THE PROLOG OF A DOCTOR RECOMMENDING ARISTOTLE.

(1)

God Almyghty save / and conferme our kyng   1   [fol. 1 a.]
  In al vertu / to his encrees of glorye   *God is called upon to endue the king with success*
His Rewm and hym / by polityk lyving
With dred and love / to have memorye
Of his Enmyes / Conquest and victorye ;   5
  With sceptre and swerd / twen bothe to doo Ryght
  Afftir his lawes / to every maneer wyght.   7

(2)

ffirst in al vertu / to sette his governaunce   8 *and regal virtues.*
  The lord to plese / and his lawes to kepe,
And his legis / with hertly Obeyssaunce
  In pees to kepe hem / wheer they wake or slepe ;
To punysshe tyrauntys / & cherysshe hem that be meke   12
  With two cleer Eyen / of discrecyoun,
  As ye hem ffynde / of disposicyoun.   14

(3)

Them that be goode / cherysshe hem in goodnesse,   15
  And them that be / froward of Corage
Peyse the ballance / be greet Avysenesse,
  ffor love nor hate / to doon Outrage.
Set a good mene / twen yong and Old of age.   19
  Excellent prynce / this processe to Compyle   *The author excuses his*
  Takith at gre / the Rudnesse of my style.   21 *poor style.*

---

[1] Lydgate ends with stanza 213, line 1491, and then Burgh goes on to the end.

PHILOSOPHERS.   B
3 ★

(4)

[fol. 1 b.] ffirst I that am / humble Servitour 22
The writer acknowledges his imperfections, Of the kyng / with hool Affecyo*u*n,
Voyde of Elloquence / I haue do my labour
To sette in Ordre / and execucyo*u*n
ffirst my symplesse / vndir Correccio*u*n, 26
but has endeavoured to obey the king's commands. With ryght hool herte / in al my best entent
ffor tacomplysshe / your comaundement. 28

(5)

Unto purpoos / my labour shewys, 29
I haue be besy / with greet dilligence
To fynde the book / of al good thewys,
The which is holly / entytled in sentence
ffor prudent prynces / moost digne of Reue*r*ence, 33
The title of the book Callyd Secrees / of Old philisoffres
Of more valew / than is gold in Coffres. 35

(6)

The which book / is notable of ffame 36
compiled by Aristotle Whylom compyled / by Arystotilees,
Which in sapience / of Secretees hath the name
Conveyed a mene / atwen werre and pees,
Ech thyng provyded / by vertuous encrees, 40
Set in Ordre / the tytles be wrytyng
To his disciple / of macedoyne kyng / 42

(7)

[fol. 2 a.] Callyd Alysaundre / the myghty Empe*r*our 43
for Alexander, Born by discent / Iustly to Succede,
With tweyne Crownys / as trewe Enherytour
Afftir his ffadir / to Regne in perce and mede,
heir of Philip of Macedon. Callyd philippus / pleynly as I Rede, 47
Thorugh al grece / namyd lord and Sire,
And by Conquest / hold the hool Empyre. 49

(8)

This Alysaundre / the Crowne whan he took, 50
Knyghtly dispoosyd / of herte and of Corage.
In whoos worshepe / compyled was this book
By Arystotyl / whanne he was falle in Age,
Had set asyde / by vertu al Outrage, 54

The Praises of Aristotle.

Inpotent to / Ryden and to travaylle;
ffor febylnesse / to counsayl in batoylle.   56

(9)
With Alisaundre / preferryd in his dayes,   57 *The praises of Aristotle,*
Was noon so greet / in his Oppynyo*u*n,
He was so trewe / fo*u*nde at al assayes,
prudent and wys / and of discrecyo*u*n,   *his prudence,*
And moost withal / of Reputacyo*u*n :   61
Grettest clerk / in Grece thoo present,
And moost Sotyl / of Entendement.   63

(10)
And with al this / his Occupacyo*u*n   64 [fol. 2 b.]
Was fully set / with entieer dilligence
And spiritual studye / of Contemplacyo*u*n.   *his studies,*
Meknesse his guyde / with moderat Reu*e*rence,
Moost charytable / al slouthe and necligence   68 *his charity,*
ffolk in myscheef / and drery to co*u*nforte ;
What eu*er*e he sauh*e* / the best to Repoorte.   70

(11)
And Specially / Set was his Reso*u*n   71
On trouthe / On feithe / and on Rightwysnesse   *his truth,*
Nat double of to*u*nge / hatyd adulacyo*u*n,
ffals Repoort / detraccyo*u*n, ydelnesse,
fforgyd talys / with oute sekirnesse,   75
And moore in vertu / hym to magneffye,
With a spirit / endewyd of p*r*ophecye.   77 *a prophet moreover.*

(12)
Had in his tyme / prerogatyves two   78
ffor his singuleer / vertuous excellence,
Callyd philisoffre / and p*r*ophete also ;
Thorugh al Grece / had moost in Reu*e*rence,
And for his gracious / Celestial inffluence   82
Bookys Recoorde / an A*u*ngel was do*u*n sent,   *Angelic visits,*
ffro god above / brought hym this present /   84

(13)
That he shulde / the book Reherse kan,   85 [fol. 3 a.]
ffor his merytes / and vertuous dignite
Be callyd an A*u*ngel / Rathere than a man

The Success of his Pupil.

<ul style="list-style:none">
<li>ffor many myracles / of Antiquite,   89</li>
<li>Vnkouth and straunge / and merveyllous to se,</li>
<li>Which surmounte / by Recoord of scrypture,</li>
<li>Both witt of man / and werkys of nature.   91</li>
</ul>

(14)

            It is also / of hym maad mencyoun,   92
As this stoory / pleynly doth expresse
ffor his vertuous / dysposicyoun
Groundid on god / Celestial of swetnesse,
In whoos memorye / wryters bere witnesse   96

taken up to heaven.   He was Ravysshed / Contemplatyff of desir
Vp to the hevene / lyk a dowe of ffyr.   98

(15)

Dewyd in vertu / be inspyracyoun   99
Abovyn alle othir / to his goostly avayl,

Alexander conquered the world by the aid of Aristotle's advice.   That Alysaundre / vnto subieccioun,
brought al kyngdammys / by his wys counsayl ;
And Cronyclers / in ther Rehersayl,   103
Al hool the world / put in Remembrance,
And enclyned / to his Obeyssaunce.   105

(16)

[fol. 3 b.]   To his poweer / and Regalye   106
He was Callyd kyng / and monarke of al,
And by his swerd / and famous Chevalrye,
By Aristotilees witt / in especial
Took in his hand / of goold the Round bal   110
To Occupyen / through his hih Renoun
vij. Clymatys / and Septemtryoun.   112

(17)

His unquestioned power over Arabia, Greece, Persia, and Media.   No grucchyng was / nouthir in word ne dede   113
Ageyn his Conquest / he was so soore drad.
Al Arabye / Grece / Perce and Mede
Ech thyng Obeyed / what so euere he bad,
Alle his Empryses / demenyd wern and lad   117
By thavys / breffly in sentence,
Of Arystotiles / witt and providence.   119

(18)

Ageyn his purpoos / there was noon Obstacle,   120
ffadir and prynce / of philosophye

Alexander's Letter to Aristotle.

Vndir nature wrought / many greet myracle
Wroot Epistelys / of prudent policye,
To Alysaundre / And to his Regalye,
By cleer exanple / be which he myght knowe
To governe him / both to hihe and lowe.

Aristotle wrote letters to Alexander, 124
126

(19)
Whan the kyng / his pistel has seyn,
And al the fourme / Conceyved in sentence,
To Arystotiles / he wrot thus ageyn
Of gentillesse / with greet Reuerence,
That he wolde / doon his dilligence,
Conceyue his menyng / and holly the matere
Of his Epistel / which that sewith here.

127 [fol. 4 a.]

to which Alexander replied.
131
133

here is the fourme of the Epistil that kyng Alysaundre sent to his maister Aristotiles.[1]

(20)
Reuerent ffadir / doctour of discyplyne
  moost notable / and digne of Reuerence,
Phebus the sonne / moor clerly doth nat shyne,
As the Repoort / of your expert prudence
Aforn provides / of Royal Confidence.
  In fewe teermys / I purpoose to Reherse
  Thing toold to me / towchyng the lond of perce.

134

138

Alexander describes Persia. 140

(21)
ffirst how that lond / and that Regioun,
  Alle othir Reemys / in philosophye
It doth excelle / and of hih Resoun
Is moost inventyff / expert in ech partye.
Ther noblesse / for to magneffye
  fferthest procede / by cleer entendement
  ffor tacomplysshe / the ffyn of ther entent.

141 *It excels in philosophy,*

145
147

(22)
Tencrese ther lordshippes / and have the souereynte .
Ovir alle Citees / and straunge Regiouns,
And by ther marcial / magnanymyte
To sprede a brood / ther domynacyouns.
Wher vpon / lyk our entencyouns

148 [fol. 4 b.]
especially in the arts of government.

152

[1] In margin of MS.

<table>
<tr><td>Alexander asks advice as to how to conquer Persia,</td><td>ffirst on this peple / I Cast me to be gynne
By your Avys / this perciens for to wynne.</td><td>154</td></tr>
</table>

(23)

	And here vpon / to make no dellayes,	155
	Mawgre ther myght / and ther Rebellyoun,	
and gives his own plan.	ffirst with my knyghthood / I wyl make Assayes	
	To haue al perce / in subieccyoun,	
	Abydyng Oonly / for short Conclusyoun	159
	With your lettrys / for my Inpartye	
	On this matere / pleynly to signeffye.	161

Thanswere of Aristotilees /

(24)

Aristotle compares the matter to the problems of Alchemy;	SOne Alisaundre / this matere to me is straunge, And includith / A maner of dyspayr.	162
	Peyse in thy Silff / yif it be lyght to Chaunge	
	ffirst from the Erthe / the Watir and the Ayr,	
	And parte the Ellementys / in ther sperys fayr.	166
	Whan this is doon / ferthermore in dede	
	Geyn percyens / in thy Conquest procede.	168

(25)

[fol. 5 a.]	ffirst thy purpoos / peyse it in ballaunce,	169
	Bothe in perce / and Septemtryoun:	
	Counte of ther Citees / the famous gouernaunce,	
he advises forethought,	And haue ther with / Consyderacyoun	
	Be a forsyght / and Cleer inspeccyoun.	173
	My counsayl is / towchyng the lond of perce,	
	ffroom thy purpoos / I Counsayl that thou Seece.	175

(26)

	Be gynne no thyng / with oute greet Avys,	176
	A ground of trouthe / first that it be possyble,	
and never to attempt an emprise unlikely to succeed;	And I Counsayl / yif that thou be wys fforeyn Empryses / which that be terryble, Attempte hem nat / but yif it be Credyble	180
	lykly on nature / by dysposicyoun	
	ffully taccomplysshe / thyn entencyoun.	182

(27)

	ffirst set a preef / in thy prudent avys	183
	In Esy wyse / by Attemperaunce,	

And by thy Counsayl / of philisoffres wys,   *he advises*
  To brynge hem Esyly / to good governaunce,   *reliance on good government,*
Of Oon Accoord / with oute varyaunce,   187
Vndir the wynges / of thy Royal bounte,
  Them to Cherysshe / in thy benignyte.   189
        (28)
Yiff thou thus doo / by vertuous Repeyr,   190   [fol. 5 b.]
  God shal encrese / of gracious inffluence,   *and promises God's blessing.*
And of full trust / I-brought out of dyspeyr
That ffynally / thy Royal excellence
Shal first plese god / in verray existence,   194
  And thy sogettys / of hool herte and entent
  Shall hool Obeye / to thy Comaundement.   196
        (29)
For entieer love / first groundid vpon the   197   *A kingdom founded on love is lasting.*
  Affecyoun Rootyd / on Royal confidence,
Voyde of al Chaung / and mutabilite,
Peysybly / in thy magnificence ;
As monarke / prevyd in existence,   201
  lyk thy desirs / thyn herte for to queme
  mong percyens / to were a dyademe.   203
        (30)
Thus by wryting / as made is mencyoun,   204   *By following Aristotle's advice Alexander gained Persia.*
Of Arystotyl / he gat al perce lond
With al the lordshippes / and euery Royal toun
And large Citees / maad soget to his hond.
Thus first of perce / as ye shal vndirstond,   208
  Though he be birthe / with othir londys manye
  Afftir his ffadir / was kyng of macedonye.   210

This Rubryssh rehersith name of the philisoffre Callid philip, born in parys, which was translator of this book.
        (31)

THis philisoffre / famous and notable   211   [fol. 6 a.]
  In al his dedys / prudent & ryght-wys,
Callyd phelip / avysee and tretable,
  In the Citee / brought forth of parys,   *Philip of Paris,*
And above alle / moost excellent of prys,   215
  Hadde in O thyng / souereyn avauntage,
  His tounge ffyled / expert in al language.   217   *skilled in languages,*

The Arabic Translator's Prolog.

(32)

and in Rhetoric;

In Rethoryk / he hadde experyence 218
Of eu*er*y strange / vnkouth nacyou*n*,
Thorugh his sugryd / Enspyred Elloquence,
Kowde of ther tou*n*ge / make a translacyou*n*.
Termys Appropryd / be interpretacyou*n* 222
They were so set / by dilligent labour
Of Tullius gardyn / he bar awey the fflour. 224

(33)

ffirst of hym sylff / he breffly doth exp*r*esse, 225

his diligence in seeking out mysteries.

His labour was / and his dilligence
Al his lyve / with wakir besynesse
Of Custummable / naturel providence,
Be disposicyou*n* / to have intelligence 229
Of Secre thynges / whan I was in dowte,
The hyd mysteryes / for to seke hem owte 231

(34)

232

[fol. 6 b.]
Here begins the prolog of Johannes.

In this matere / was set al myn Entent
And myn Inward / hertly attendau*n*ce
Ther-of to have / Cleer entendement,
And of scryptures / Iust Reconysau*n*ce.
To have with them / confederat Allyau*n*ce 236
I sparyd noon / What fortune did falle
Philisoffres to seke / hem Oon and alle. 238

(35)

So desirous I was / of herte and mynde, 239
With al my wittys / to serchyn and visite

He visits Arabia and India in search of wisdom.

In Arrabia / and the ferther ynde
Philisoffres that cowde / hem sylff best quite,
And Rethoryciens / to compyle and endyte 243
Vnkouth mysteryes / I was glad hem to se
By ther suppoort / to lerne Some secree. 245

(36)

I was so brent / in Cupydes ffyr 246
To knowe first / whanne I had gonne,
With hevenly fervence / Celestial of desir
To taste the licour / of Cytheroes tonne,
And knowe the cleernesse / of the bryght sonne, 250

His Search for Wisdom. 9

Which in merydyen / moost Amerously doth shyne
Breest of philisoffres / be grace tenlvmyne. 252

(37)
Whanne I had serchyd / hih*e* and lowe 253 [fol. 7a.]
  In Sundry stodyes / arid many greet lybrarye *After much fruitless search he meets a hermit,*
Of this sonne / the bryghtnesse for to knowe,
I was wery / theron for to tarye,
Tyl at the laste / I fond a solytarye 257
  Syttyng alloone / with lokkys hore and gray,
Which toward phebus / taught me the ryght way. 259 *who instructs him*

(38)
The which sonne / of bryghtnesse perlees, 260
  Compyled aforn / by an expert philisoffre,
Callyd in his tyme / Exculapides, *from the book of Æsculapius*
To whoom I gan / my seruise for to Offre,
ffor gold nor Silvir / hadde I noon to proffre. 264
  He hold hym first / be megre of Abstinence,
Whoom I besought / with devout Reu*er*ence, 266

(39)
That he wolde / goodly me Enspyre 267
  In this mat*ere* / which I haue be-gonne
Toward the weye / which I moost desire,
The goldene path / direct unto the sonne,
Wheer philisoffres / as they Reherse konne, 271
  Took ther laude / which that lastith eu*ere*
In parfight Clernesse / and may Eclypse neu*ere*. 273

(40)
Perseveraunt / in hoope whan I stood, 274 [fol. 7b.]
  Of my Request / with feithful attendaunce,
This solitarye / whan he vndirstood
Al that I mente / with eu*ery* Circumstaunce, *with perfect clearness.*
I fond in hym / no strange varyaunce 278
  To myn entent / breffly to comprehende,
In goodly wyse / he lyst to condiscende. 280

(41)
ffro poynt to poynt / taccomplysshe my desirs, 281
  Stood in greet hoope / it shulde me prevaylle
fforthryd in the weye / wheer phebus moost cleer is,

The Translator's Prolog.

  Voyde of dispeyr / be-Cause my travaylle
  Was expleyted / that no thyng did faylle.   285
  Cleer was the sonne / Watir, Erthe, and Eyer,
  With which graunt / moost glad in my Repayer.   287

(42)

  Gretly Reioysshed / both of cheer and fface,   288
  And Renewyd / with a glad Corage,

So he returned, thanking God, to translate this book
  Retournyd ageyn / to myn owne place,
  Gaf thank to god / to my greet avauntage,
  That he me gaff / so fortunat passage   292
  In short tyme / and in so short a date
  This seyd book / at leyser to translate   294

(43)

[fol. 8 a.]
  With greet studye / tacomplysshe the byddyng,   295
  And to procede / in the translacyoun
  Of this book / moost notable in wrytyng
  Of Royal materis / souereyn of Renoun,
  Which as monarcha / of euery Regioun,   299
  Gaff me this Charge / knelyng on my kne

from Greek into Chaldee and Arabic.
  It to translate / fro greek in to Chalde.   301

here the Translator resortith ageyn to set in a prologe, on this wyse.[1]

(44)

  I gan Remembre / and muse in my Resoun,   302
   A Sodeyn consceyt / fyl in my ffantasye,
  And made a stynt / in my translacyoun

Lydgate here describes
  A twix two / stood in Iupartye
  To what party / my penne I shulde applye.   306
  Thus in a dowte / kowde nat my Sylff counforte
  Till I a brayde / in purpoos to Resorte   308

(45)

  To hym that drough / this processe moost devyne,   309

the person by whom the Latin translation was made,
  Callyd in his tyme / in philoosophye
  Sonne, merour / and launpe tenlvmyne
  This translacyoun / of Royal policye
  Out of Greek / and tounge of Arrabye   313
  In to latyn / a Celestial werk
  At Request / of this notable Clerk.   315

[1] In margin of MS.

Dedication of the Latin Translation. 11

(46)
Which in thoo dayes / was of greet dignite,   316   [fol. 8 b.]
Bysshop Sacryd / in the Citee Covalence,   *for Guy, bishop of Valence,*
Metropolitan / of moost Auctoryte,
By whoos Consayl / and in whoos Reuerence
A philisoffre / expert in ech science,   320
Callyd liberales / that been in nownbre sevene,
Namyd phillipus / myn Auctour doth hym nevene.   322

(47)
Which took vpon hym / this vertuous labour   323   *Philip of Paris,*
Vndir the wynges / of humble Obedyence,
That he of grace / wolde doon hym this ffavour,
This hooly Guydo / ffamous in ech science,
In whoos wurschepe / and in whoos Reuerence   327   *whose epistle dedicatory to the Latin version*
By whoos byddyng / as he vndirtook,
Wroot to hym thus / the prologe of this book.   329   *begins here.*

(48)
Vndir your benigne / gracious suppoort,   330
Twen hoope and dreed / Astonyd in my Symplesse,
ffor my moost vertuous / and Singuleer counfort,
With an exordye / groundid on meknesse,
With quakyng penne / my consceyt to expresse,   334
ffor lak of Rhethoryk / feerful to vnffoolde
To your noblesse / to wryten as I wolde.   336

(49)
I have no Colour / but Oonly Chalk and sable,   337   [fol. 9 a.]
To peynte or portreye / lyst that I shulde Erre   *The bishop's fame,*
Your hih Renoun / which is in-comperable ;
Your hoolynesse / it spredith out so ferre,
lych as the moone / passith a smal sterre :   341
So your vertues / Reche vp to the hevene,
To Arthurus / And the sterrys sevene.   343

(50)
And as phebus / with his bryght beemys,   344
The goldene wayn / thorugh the world doth lede,
ffrom Est tyl West / with his celestial streemys
In merydien / fervent as the glede,
Bove moone and sterrys / in cleernesse [1]doth excede ;[1]   348
     [1–1] not in MS.

The Virtues and Praises

<small>virtues,</small>

And semblaby / al men seyn the same,
The vertues sprede / of your good name. 350

(51)

In sondry konnynges / I Can Remembre noon, 351
And I shulde / Reherse hem Ceryously,

<small>knowledge.</small> But ye haue parcel / of hem eu*er*ychoon,
And shokkyd hem vp / in Ordre by and by;
And lyk myn Auctour / I dar seyn trewly, 355
And Repoorte / as it Comyth to mynde
In my translacyo*un* / to seyn ryght as I ffynde. 357

(52)

<small>[fol. 9 b.]</small> ffirst with Noe / ye have exp*er*t prudence, 358
<small>He is compared to Noah, Abraham, Isaac, Jacob, Joshua,</small>
With Abraham / feith, trouthe, and Equite;
With Isaak / prevyd conffydence,
And with Iacob / longanymyte;
Stabylnesse / with hardy Iosue, 362
Tretable abydyng / Reknyd in substau*n*ce;
<small>Moses,</small> With duk Moyses / long perseverau*n*ce. 364

(53)

<small>Elijah,</small> With helye / parfight devocyo*un*, 365
<small>David,</small> Of Dauid / the grete benygnyte,
<small>Elisha,</small> Of Elyseus / expert perfeccyo*un*,
<small>Solomon, Daniel, Job,</small> Witt of Salamon / with Danyel Chastite;
Suffrance of Iob / in his Infirmyte, 369
<small>Isaiah,</small> Plente of language / with hooly Isaye,
<small>Jeremiah,</small> And lamentacio*un*s / expert in Ieremye. 371

(54)

And as your ffame / beryth Cleer witnesse, 372
Ye haue also / with polityk prudence
<small>Cicero and</small> In worldly thynges / greet avysenesse,
Circu*n*spect / and vertuous dilligence,
And with Tullius / sugryd Elloquence: 376
The Repoort goth Est / West, North, and South,
<small>Homer.</small> Callyd Omerus / with the hony mouth. 378

(55)

<small>[fol. 10 a.]</small> With alle these vertues / plentevous in lecture, 379
<small>His episcopal virtues,</small> Saddest exa*u*nple / prevyd in sobirnesse,
Day and nyght / moost wakir in scripture,

of Guido, Bishop of Valence:

Bryght as the sonne / day sterre of hoolynesse;
In moral vertues / Al vices to Represse, 383
Callyd Aurora / of spiritual doctryne,
Namely in mateerys / hevenly and divyne. 385

(56)
Ye wer of lyff / Egal with hooly Seyntes, 386 *and holy life.*
In parfight prayer / and Contemplacyo*u*n,
fful Offte wepte / and made your compleyntes
ffor Synfful wrecchys / in desolacio*u*n,
Disconsolat / in trybulacyo*u*n, 390
That fro grace / and al vertu exyled,
Ye wern ay besy / tyl they were Reconcyled. 392

(57)
By your dilligence / notable instruccyo*u*n, 393
ffro vicious lyff / ther corages to declyne, *How he improved the wicked.*
And Race awey / al fals Occasyo*u*n
Which ageyn vertu / shulde brynge hem to Rwyne,
ffor gracious phebus / that doth alwey shyne 397
To forthre yow / in spiritual avayl,
Was Alwey pr*e*sent / to been of your Co*u*nsayl. 399

(58)
In liberal science / that be sevene in no*u*nbre, 400 [fol. 10 *b*.]
Your studye ay stood / and your dilligence *His knowledge of the 7 sciences,*
bryght as Apollo / with oute shadwe or Owmbre,
ffor your cleer shynyng / was soth in existence,
Voyde of al pallyd / or Contirfeet Apparence, 404
Outward in Cheer / of pryde was no signe, *and humility withal.*
And in your poort / to alle folk moost benygne. 406

(59)
And for ye wer / moost famous in science, 407
Conveyed by grace / and with humylite,
Wheer eu*e*re ye wern / Abydyng in pr*e*sence, *To know him was a liberal education.*
Men seyd ther was / An Vnyue*r*site
To yow entytled / of Antiquite, 411
As it was / Repoortyd in substau*n*ce,
To yow appropryd / be goddys Ordynau*n*ce, 413

(60)
With Addicio*u*n / of the hevenly inffluence. 414
ffor in your tyme / was no Creature

That was expert / nor preferryd in sentence,
To be comparyd / nor of lecture
To your noblesse / and favour of nature 418
Was nat set bak / but lykly to contvne,
be god and grace / and favour of ffortune, 420

(61)

[fol. 11 a.] So to perseuere / and lastyn a long date, 421
Prayers for his long life.
God lyst your yeerys / for to multiplye
Grace from abovyn / and your dispoosyd fate
At the sevene / wellys of philosophye,
With Crystallyn sprynges / Ran to ech partye, 425
That the swetnesse / of the soote streemys
Ther lycour shadde / in to alle Reemys. 427

(62)

I lakke language / breffly for to telle 428
The bawme vpclosyd / in your tresourye,
He had studied Lucan, Homer, and Virgil;
Which that ye drank / at Elyconys welle,
With lucan, Omer / foundours of poetrye,
And virgile / which had the Regalye, 432
Callyd in his tyme / the singuleer Crownyd man,
Above al othir / Poete mantvan. 434

(63)

Ye bar the keye / of the Secre Coffre, 435
Callyd Registrer / of ther tresoury,
he was a philosopher and a poet.
With two prerogatives / first a philisoffre,
And moost expert / your tyme in poetrye,
And yif I shal / breffly Speceffye 439
Your hihe merytes / and your magnificence
by Iugement yove / direct to your Clemence. 441

(64)

[fol. 11 b.] This book in Grece / was brought to your sight 442
This book had been given him in Antioch,
In Antioche / your noblesse to delyte,
As a Charbouncle / ageyn dirknesse of nyght;
O Rychest Rubye / Or clerest margaryte
Of philisoffres / and pleynly for to wryte, 446
Sent of Assent / in their Oppynyoun
That ye therof / shulde have inspeccyoun. 448

from the Arabic to be made.

(65)
Off entent / it shulde be translatyd 449
ffrom Arabyk / to moor pleyn language,
ffor latyn is moore pleyn / and moore dylatyd
In al nacyouns / to Oold and yong of Age;
And for I wolde / of herte and hool Corage 453
Obeye your byddyng / of humble Affeccyoun
I took vpon me / this Translacyoun. 455

and was translated from Arabic into Latin by his orders, since Latin was generally known.

(66)
To Condiscende / in al my best entent 456
In this matere / my labour for to shewe,
ffirst taccomplyshhe / your Comaundement
Yit wer me loth / Ovir myn hed to hewe,
But for ther been / of Copyes but a fewe 460
Of this book / Reknyd in sentence,
To doo yow plesaunce / and also Reuerence. 462

Very few copies of the book exist;

(67)
I took vpon me / your disciple and Clerk, 463 [fol. 12 a.]
As I Cowde / vndir Correccioun,
To procede and gynne / vpon this werk,
Out of Arabyk / with hool affeccyoun,
Into latyn / make this Translacyoun, 467
Oonly tagreen / with al humylite,
To your moost famous / magnanymyte. 469

but the translator on his orders will do his best:

(68)
Nat woord by woord / Cause of varyaunce, 470
In this tonges / ther is greet difference;
But lyk my Symple / vnexpert suffysaunce,
ffolwyn myn Auctour / in menyng and sentence,
Ryght of hool herte / and entieer dilligence, 474
As Arystotiles / Rehersyth by wrytyng
In his Epistil / to Alisaundre kyng. 476

not a literal translation, since the languages are so different.

here folowith the secund pistil that kyng Alysaundre
sent to his maistir Aristotiles.[1]

(69)
WHan Alisaundre / as is Rehersyd heer, 477
this philisoffre / for vertues many-foold,

[1] In margin of MS.

A List of Aristotle's Secret Crafts.

<small>Aristotle unable by reason of age to go to Alexander.</small>

Sent unto hym / a secre massageer,
With-oute Exskus / to come to his houshoold;
But he ageyn / for he was feble and Oold, 481
And inpotent / on the tothir syde,
And vnweldy / for to goon or Ryde. 483

(70)

[fol. 12 b.] But cheef cause / why Alisaundre sente 484
A purpoos take / and a fantasye
To declare pleynly / what he mente;

<small>Alexander, very desirous of knowing Aristotle's secrets;</small>

He wyst in soth / that in philosophye,
With othir secretys / of Astronomye, 488
He was expert / and moost cowde vndirstonde,
This was in cheef Cause / of the kynges sonde. 490

(71)

<small>which were— Astrology,</small>
Poweer of planetys / And mevyng of al sterrys, 491
And of euery / hevenly intelligence,
Disposicioun / of pees and ek of werrys,
And of ech othir / straunge hyd science

<small>Magic,</small>
As the sevene goddys / by ther Inffluence, 495
Dispoose the Ordre / of Incantaciouns,

<small>Alchemy,</small>
Or of Sevene metallys / the transmutaciouns, 497

(72)

<small>Calculations, and Geomancy;</small>
With othir Crafftys / which that be secre, 498
Calculacioun / and Geomancye,

<small>the arts of Circe and Medea; Physiognomy, Pyromancy, and Geometry.</small>
Difformacyouns / of Circes and meede,
lokyng of ffacys / and piromancye,
On lond and watir / Crafft of Geometrye, 502
Heyhte and depnesse / with al experience,
Therfore the kyng / desyryd his presence. 504

(73)

[fol. 13 a.] But for al thys / with Inne hym Sylff a thyng, 505

<small>Aristotle kept back some secrets:</small>
Ther was a Secre / he kept nat do discloose,
Nor to puplysshe / Opynly to the kyng,
Takyng exaunple / by two thynges in a Roose;
ffirst how the fflour / greet swetnesse doth dispoose, 509
Yit in the thorn / men fynde greet sharpnesse;
And thus in konnyng / ther may been a lyknesse. 511

(74)

In herbe & fflour / in wryting woord and stoon,   512   he wished to keep secrets from the people,
Ech hath his vertu / of god and of nature,
But the knowyng / is hyd fro many Oon,
And nat declaryd / to euery Creature ;   516
Wherfore he Cast / twen Resoun and mesure
To shape a weye / bothe the kyng to plese,   and yet to please the king.
Somwhat to vncloose / and sette his herte at Ese.   518

(75)

Ther is of ryght / a greet difference   519
Twen a prynces / Royal dignite
And atwen Comouns / Rude intelligence,   The common people should not try to learn things
To whoom nat longith / to medle in no degre
Of konnynges / that shulde be kept secre ;   523
ffor to a kynges / famous magnificence,   which belong only to kings and clerks.
And to Clerkys / which haue experience,   525

(76)

It cordith wel / to serche Out scrypture,   526   [fol. 18 b.]
Misteryes hyd / of fowlys, beeste, and tree,   Lydgate here tells of the mysteries of nature.
And of Aungellys / moost sotyl of nature,
Of mynerall / and fysshes in the see,
And of stoonys / Specially of three—   530   The three stones— Mineral, Vegetative,
Oon myneral / Anothir vegetatyff,
Partyd on foure / to lengthe a mannys lyff.   532

(77)

Of which I Radde / among othir stoonys   533
Ther was Oon / was Callyd Anymal,   and Animal ;
ffoure Ellementys / wrought Out for the noonys—   the last made from the 4 elements in equal proportions.
Erthe, Watir, and Eyr / And in Especial
Ioyned with ffyr / proporcyoun maad Egal ;   537
And I dar seyn / breffly, and nat tarye,
Is noon suych stoon / ffound in the lapydarye.   539

(78)

I Rad Oonys / in a philisoffre,   540   It will cure sickness of all kinds.
Ageyn ech Syknesse / of valew doth moost Cure ;
Al the tresour / and gold in Cresus coffre,
Nor al the stoonys / that growe be nature,
Wrought by Crafft / or forgid by picture,   544
PHILOSOPHERS.

Lydgate warns the Ignorant and Foolish

    lapis et non lapis / stoon of grettest fame,
Aristotiles / gaf it the same name.   546

(79)

[fol. 14 a.]
The translator's incapacity

And for I haue / but litel Rad or seyn,   547
   To wryte or medle / of so hih materys,
ffor presumpcyoun / somme wolde haue disdeyn
   To be so boold / or Clymbe in my disirys,
   To scale the laddere / above the nyne sperys,   551
   Or medle of Rubyes / that yeve so cleer a lyght
On hooly shrynes / in the dirk nyght.   553

(80)

for dealing with the subject.

I was nevir / noon expert Ioweler,   554
   In suych materys / to putte my Sylff in prees
With philisoffres / myn Eyen wer nat Cleer,
   Nouthir with plato / nor with Socratees,

Aristotle taught Alexander,

   Except the Prynce / Aristotilees,   558
   Of philisoffres / to Alisaundre kyng
Wrot of this stoon / the merveylle in[1] werkyng,   560

(81)

as in a parable,

In prevy wyse / lych to his Ententys,   561
   Secretys hyd / Cloos in philosophie;

how to separate each of the 4 elements, how to purify them, and how to combine them again.

ffirst departyng / of the foure Ellementys,
   And afftirward / as he doth speceffye
Euerych of hem / for to Recteffye;   565
   And afftir this / lyk his Oppynyoun,
Off this foure / make a Coniunccyoun.   567

(82)

[fol. 14 b.]

And[2] In suych wyse / performe vp this stoon,   568
   Seen in the Ioynyng / ther be noon Outrage;
But the fals Erryng / hath fonnyd many Oon,
   And brought hem afftir / in ful greet Rerage,

What expenses are incurred by the ignorant in their search for the stone;

By expensys / and Outragious Costage;   572
   ffor lak of brayn / they wern maad so wood
Thyng to be-gynne / which they nat vndirstood.   574

(83)

ffor he that lyst / put in experience,   575
   fforboode Secrees / I holde hym but a fool,
lyk hym that temptith / of wylful necligence,

    [1] 'in al' MS.   [2] Not in MS.

of the Cost of the Study of Alchemy.

To stonde vp ryght / On a thre foot stool,
Or sparyth a stewe / and fyssheth a bareyn pool : 579
  When al is doon / he get noon othir grace,   *and what*
  Men wyl scorne hym / and mokke his foltyssh fface. 581 *reward they obtain.*

(84)
It is no Crafft / poore men tassaye, 582
It Causith Coffres / and Chestys to be bare,   *How poor men fare.*
Marryth wyttes / and braynes doth Affraye ;
  Yit be wryting / this book doth declare,
  And be Resouns / lyst nat for to spare, 586
    With goldeyn Resouns / in taast moost lykerous,
    Thyng per ignotum / prevyd per ignocius. 588

(85)
Title of this book / labor philosoph*orum*, 589 [fol. 15 a.]
  Namyd also / de Regimine principum,
Of philisoffres / secreta secret*orum*,
  Tresour compyled / *omni*um virtutum,
  Rewle directorye / set up in a somme,[1] 593
    As Complexio*uns* / in helthe and syknesse,
    Dispose them sylff / to mornyng or to gladnesse. 595

(86)
The which book / direct to the kyng 596
  Alisaundre / bothe in werre and pees,
lyk his Request / and Royal Comaundyng,
  fful A-Complysshed / by Aristotiles,
  ffeble for Age / and inpotent douteles, 600
    Hool of Corage / and trewe in his entent,
    Tobeye his byddyng / this book he to hym sent. 602

To telle of hy*m* the Genealogie which t*r*anslated this book.

(87)
HE that first / this labour vndirtook, 603
  Was Callyd Iohn / And of nacyoun   *Johannes*
A spaynol born / which began this book,
  Of eu*er*y tou*n*ge / And eu*er*y Regioun ;
  he was expert / as maad is mencio*un*, 607
    To speke ther language / myn Auctour tellith thus,
    And Callyd sone / of Oon patricius. 609 *son of Patricius,*

[1] MS. 'sonne.'

The Prolog of Johannes Hispalensis.

(88)

[fol. 15 b.] Trewe expert / and dilligent to konne, 610
mong philisoffres / put ay hym Sylff in prees,
who came to the Oracle of the Sun, built by Æsculapius, Cam to Oraculum / Callyd of the sonne,
A place bylt / by Esculapides,
Wheer tabyde / his Restyng place he chees, 614
Thoughte he wolde / for a sesoun tarye,
and found a hermit there; Cause that he fond / A persone solitarye. 616

(89)

Dempte he was brought / thedir by myracle, 617
and after much entreaty was taught, In lowly wyse / besought hym On his kne
To vouchesauf / to shewe in that Oracle
hyd merveylles / which ther wer kept Secre;
And of Affeccioun / and gracious pite, 621
I ffond hym goodly / and benigne of Cheer,
My Requestys / at leyser for to heer. 623

(90)

And whanne I hadde / with oute more Obstacle, 624
and given this book of Secrets, Seyn ther thynges / with Secrees delitable,
That wer divyne / and Cloos in that Oracle,
It was a paradys / verray incomparable:
And for this philisoffre / was so mercyable 628
Towardys me / and shewyd no dysdeyn,
Thankyng my maister / Retournyng hoom ageyn. 630

(91)

[fol. 16 a.] Afftir this labour / I gan dispoose me 631
which he translated from Greek through Syriac into Arabic. To procede / on this translacyoun,
Out of greek tounge / and language Chalde,
To Arabyk afor / of hool entencyoun,
That I myght / for short conclusyoun, 635
lyk my desir / tacomplysshe and confoorme,
This pistil to wryte / vndir this same foorme. 637

Here is the Epistil of the translator.

(92)

IN the name of Arystotiles 638
Wel avysed / A processe to provide;
In his exskus / he was nat Rekkelees,

The Second Letter of Aristotle to Alexander. 21

But Inpotent / for to goon or Ryde, Aristotle, unable to come
And Alleggyng / on the tothir syde, 642 to the king, sends him a letter
The kynges lettres / he wel vndirstood, of advice,
Which for to Obeye / herte and wyl wer good. 644

(93)
Yif inpotence / of his vnweldy age, 645
In his desirs / put hym nat abak,
To goon or Ryde / to lettyn his passage,
Hool in his wyl / ther was nevir lak,
Though his heer / was tournyd whyte fro blak; 649
Besought hym lowly / of his Royal grace, excusing himself,
To take a leyser / competent and space, 651

(94)
In his exskus / this pistil to vncloose; 652 [fol. 16 b.]
And first Advertise / in Especial,
Witt and Corage / and hym Silff dispoose,
To leve al manerys / that be bestial,
Vertues to folwe / that been Inperyal; 656
This to seyne / first prudently discerne, and teaching the arts of
Twen vice and vertu / his peple to governe. 658 kingcraft.

(95)
Off his pistil / a breef Subcrypcyoun, 659
Set lowly vndir / to god lefft vp his cheer,
And of hool herte / makyng this Orysoun
ffor Alysaundre / And this was his preyeer: His prayer on Alexander's
"God that sit hihest / Above the sterrys cleer, 663 behalf against sloth,
Grant first our kyng / tavoyde from hym slouthe,
A fals stepmodir / And thanne begynne at trouthe." 665 for truth,

(96)
And of thy Counsayl / make hire cheef pryncesse, 666
That she may provide / And takyn hede
With outyn handys / by greet avysenesse,
Outhir for favour / or for Old hatrede,
Chace flatererys / and hem that take mede, 670 against flatterers
And suych tounges / of Custom that be double, and double tongues;
And namely them / that Can sowe trouble. 672

(97)
Whysperyng tounges / of taast moost serpentyn, 673 [fol. 17 a.]
Silvir scalyd / whoos mouth is ful of blood,

<small>Aristotle likens flatterers to serpents</small>

Smothe afore folk / to fawnyn and to shyne,
And shewe two facys / in Oon hood ;
Ther sugre is soote / ther galle doth no good,   677
Alle suych shulde / be voyded from Counsayl :

<small>and to bees.</small>

A bee yevith hony / and styngeth with the tayl.   679

(98)

<small>He advises Alexander to disregard their counsel,</small>

This forseyd peple / togidere to Combyne,   680
Which be froward / of ther Condiciouns,
Though that they been / discendid of Oon lyne,
Trouthe wyl nat folwe / ther Oppynyouns ;
ffor vnto Royal / disposicyouns,   684
As I seyd Erst / Avoyde fro the slouthe,
And Cheef of uertues / set in hir place trouthe.   686

(99)

And to directe / lyk myn Oppynyoun,   687
Whan thou hast voyded / slouthe and necligence,
And trouthe is entryd / with discrecyoun,
And Conveyed / to¹ thy magnificence,

<small>and to listen only to truth.</small>

I trust ye shal / yeve hem Audience   691
In myn exskus / which in philisoffye
be Callyd ffadir / and in prophecye /   693

(100)

    694

[fol. 17 b.] Have a spirit / to forn of knowlechyng.
In your service / whan I first began,
Declaryd mysteryes / of the hevenly kyng,
Which excelle Resoun / and wit of man,

<small>Aristotle had been visited by an angel,</small>

And how the lord / As I Reherse Can   698
ffor your sake / Sent an Aungel doun
moo to enspyre / by Revelacyoun.   700

(101)

    701

As it is / Repoortyd in scripture,

<small>and taken up to heaven, as Greek books show.</small>

In Grekyssh bookys / Above the sterryd hevene,
Arystotiles / was Aungelyk of nature,
ffadir and ffoundour / of the sciencys sevene,
Reysed in a pyleer / wrought of ffyry leveue,   705
So hih aloffte / be Revelacyoun,
Knew hevenly secretys / At his comyng doun.   707

¹ 'to hym' in MS.

Aristotle promises to disclose all Secrets. 23

(102)

By whoos Counsayl / in Arrabye folk Carpe,   708   Vows on the peacock of Alexander's chivalry.
Hadde of sevene / Clymatys domynacyoun,
Of al the world / Emperour and monarke,
Ynde, Ethiope / and euery nacyoun :
And greete porrus / be poweer he Cast don,   712
Vowes of the pecock / doon be dayes Olde
wern a-Complysshed / by his knyghtes bolde.   714

(103)   [fol. 18 a.]

Ther be secrees / of materys hih and lowe,   715
Hyd in nature / Concelyed and Secre,
Which Alisaundre / desired for to knowe
By Aristotiles / a certeyn prevyte
Nat speceffyed / Cloos in hym Sylff kept he,   719
Which was delayed / Of greet providence,
Tyl he hym sylff / come to his presence.   721

(104)

Nnevirtheles / at Ellyconys welle,   722
This philisoffre / by fulsom habundaunce,
Drank grettest plente / which hym lyst nat telle ;   Aristotle discovered his secrets under cover
I mene secretys / moost souereyn of plesaunce,
Which to discure / or wryte hem in substaunce,   726   of dark sayings.
lyk his desirs / to servyn his entent,
I shal so doon / he shal be ful content.   728

(105)

By a manere / lyknesse and ffigure,   729
Dirk Outward / mysty for to se,
lyk a thyng / that were above nature,
As it were seyd / in Enigmate,
Touchyd a parcel / I mene thus parde   733
As vndir Chaaf / is Closyd pure Corn,   End of the prologs.
Touchyd somdel / in partye heer-to-forn.   735

Of foure maner kynges diuers of disposicion.   [fol. 18 b.]

(106)

THer be kynges / dispoosyd by nature,   736   Kings considered from the point of view of their largesse;
Somme that broyde / on liberallyte,
And of hool herte / with al ther besy Cure

Kings should neither be

the king who is careful of his reputation for liberality;

Ther studye set / in largesse to be fre,
  That ther Imperial / magnanymyte 740
  Shulde nat be spottyd / in no maner wyse,
  Towchyng the vice / of froward Coveityse. 742

(107)

the king generous to himself and his subjects;

The philisoffre / in Ordre doth expresse, 743
  That som kyng / to hym sylff is large,
  And to his sogettys / shewith greet largesse,

the king generous to his subjects and not to himself. The Italian opinion;

And som kyng streyght / to take On hym the Charge
  largely to parte / and haue hym Sylff Skarce; 747
  But ytalyens / Recorde be Wrytyng
  large on ech party / is vertuous in a kyng. 749

(108)

the Indian opinion;

Aristotiles / writt of them in ynde, 750
  They Repoorte / that kyng is gloryous,
  Which to hym Sylff / is most skars of kynde,
  And to his sogettys / is large and plentevous;[1]

the Persian opinion;

Yit they of perce / be Contraryous: 754
  But to my doom / that kyng that hath the Charge
  Is moost Comendid / that is to bothe large. 756

(109)[2]

[fol. 19 a.]

the translator's opinion.

I mene as thus / by a dyvisioun 757
  Toward hym sylff / kepe his Estat Royal
  By attemperaunce / and by discrecioun,
  lyk his sogettys / in Especial,
  As they disserve / to be liberal, 761
  Twen moche and lyte / A mene to devise
  Of to mekyl / And streight Coveitise. 763

(110)

A difference between prodigality and munificence;

Ther is a maner / straunge difference, 764
  ffor lak of Resoun / twen prodigalyte
  And in a kynges / Royal magnificence,
  Whan he lyst parte / of liberallite
  To his sogettys / as they been of degre 768
  So Egally / I-holdyn the ballaunce,
  Ech man contente / with discreet Suffysaunce. 770

---

[1] 59 Ar. omits from line 753 to line 759.
[2] Not in 2251 Harl.

Avaricious nor Prodigal.

(111)

Ther is a mene / peysed in ballaunce 771
Atwixen hym / that is a greet wastour — wasting and
To kepe a meene / by attemperaunce,
That ech thyng / be peysed be mesour,
That foltyssh grucchyng / bryng in noon Errour, 775 grudging.
Considred first / of prynces the poweer,
And next the merytes / of the laboureer. 777

(112)

Concludyng thus / twen good wyl and grucchyng 778 [fol. 19 b.]
Of them that been / feithful of servyse, Consider-
And of anothir / froward and grucchyng, ation must
That wyl Obeye / in no maneer wyse, be taken of
To folwe the doctryne / and the greet Empryse, 782 the merit of
To putte his body / in pereel / moost mortal, the recipient.
And in Iupartyes / that be marcial. 784

(113)

To alle suych / A prynce of hihe noblesse 785 To whom to
Shal nat spare / his gold / nor his tresour be liberal.
To parte with hem / Stuff of his Rychesse,
Thing Apropryd / to every Conquerour.
But yif ffredam / Conduite his labour, 789
That liberallyte / his Conquest doo provide, The danger
At his moost nede / his men wyl nat abyde. 791 of illiberality.

(114)

Aristotiles / made a discripcyoun 792
fful notable / in his wrytynges,
Sette a maneer / of divysyoun,
That ther be / dyuers maneer kynges;
Somme be large / in ther departynges 796 A king
To bothe tweyne / Seith he is moost good should pro-
That atwen tweyne / trewly yevith his good. 798 self and his
subjects.

(115)

But he that is / streyght in his kepyng, 799 [fol. 20 a.]
lokkith vp his tresour / in his Coffre,
And lyst nat parte / with no maner thyng
With his sogettys / nor no good to proffre
In nede or myscheef / lyst no part to Offre; 803 A covetous,
sparing king.

I Can nat seyn / his ffredam to Comende,
That vnto nouthir / lyst nat to entende. 805

(116)

Praises of a munificent king,

A kyng that partyth / suych as god hath sent 806
Be fortune / Or Conquest in batuylle,
To his knyghtes / or sowdiours of entent,
Suych at moost nede / in trouthe may avaylle,
And them Relevith / that be falle in poraylle, 810
What folwith afftir / breffly to termyne,
lyght of his noblesse / shal euere encreese & shyne. 812

(117)

Nature hath set / tweyne extremytees; 813
ffirst be a maneer / discreet providence,
That the streemys / of liberallite

and of a wise

Set in good mesour / Reffreytes of prudence,
Peysed in ballaunce / So that Sapience, 817
Queen of vertues / as lady souereyne,
That suych a meene / be set atwen hem tweyne. 819

(118)

[fol. 20 b.] ffirst conceyved / and peysed ech Estat, 820
That ther be no / froward transgressyoun
Of wylfulnesse / nor no froward debat,

and prudent one.

Ech thyng in Ordre / Conveyed by Resoun
That mesour haue / domynacyoun, 824
As it is ryght / of trouthe and Equite,
Twen Avaryce / and prodigalyte. 826

(119)

And whoo that wyl / breeffly in sentence 827
Trewly devyde / vertuous largesse,
ffroom hym hath no / polityk Aduertence,
Them to governe / of Royal gentillesse,
I dar wel seyn / breffly and expresse, 831
Of good Repoort / shortly determyne

His glory shall shine

his sonne of vertues / thorugh the world shal shyne 833

(120)

without eclipse or detraction.

With oute Eclypsyng / of Ony mystes blake 834
Or fals Repoort / of ony dirk shours,[1]
Or froward tounges / that noyse or sclaundre make,

[1] 59 Ar. and Harl. 2251 omit from line 835 to line 841.

To medle netlys / with soote Roose flours :
laureer Crownys / be maad for Conquerours 838
In tryvmphes / trewly for to deme
Whoo is moost wourthy / to were a dyademe. 840

(121)
A kyng dispoosyd / of Royal excellence, 841 [fol. 21 a.]
ffirst to be large / cheefly in thynges tweyne,
large to hym Sylff / And ffre in his dyspence,
Twen moche, litel / that wysdam to Ordeyne,
That discrecyoun / As lady Sovereyne, 845 *A discreet king shares his largesse*
With Resoun present / At good leyseer tabyde,
That hasty wyl / medle on nouthir syde; 847

(122)
Streyght to hym Sylff / in suych maneer wyse, 848
Aforn Considred / his magnanymyte,
That Royal ffredam / dispoose So the Assyse
Toward his liges / that suych Repoort may be,
To kepe the ffraunchyse / of liberallyte, 852
Twen his noblesse / and his liges bothe, *between the noblesse and his subjects.*
In so good meene / that nouthir of hem be wrothe. 854

(123)
They of ytallye / in ther Oppynyoun, 855
Seyn / it was / no vice in a kyng,
Yif he be large / be distrubucyoun
To them that been / vndir hym levyng;
But they of perce / Recorde in ther wryting, 859
He that is large / vnto bothe two,
ffirst to hym Sylff / and lige men Also. 861

(124)
But to my doom / and to my ffantasye, 862 [fol. 21 b.]
Seith Aristotiles / that kyng is moost comendable
That hath largesse / in his Regalye,
With good meenys / in vertu stonde stable,
Trewe in his feith / not feynt nor varyable, 866
Twen Avaryce / of trouthe and Equite,
The vice avoyding / of prodigalyte. 868

(125)
Breffly the vertu / of Royal hih largesse, 869 *Aristotle commends the mean between avarice and prodigality.*
Set in A meene / of prudent governaunce,

28 *Princes should beware of Flatterers,*

<small>How largesse should be apportioned.</small> That ther be nouthir / skarsete nor excesse,
But a ryght Rewle / of Attemperaunce;
So that mesour / weye the ballaunce, 873
To Recompense / of Equite and Ryght,
lyk ther merytes / to euery maneer wyght. 875

(126)

<small>The evils arising from flatterers.</small> Atwen trouthe / And forgyd fflaterye 876
Ther is a straunge / vnkouth difference,
Contraryous poysoun / I dar wel certeffye,
To alle Estatys / of Royal excellence:
Wheer double menyng / hath ony existence, 880
Ther growith ffrawde / And Covert fals poysoun,
And sugryd galle / honyed with Collusyoun. 882

(127)

[fol. 22 a.] Off Prynces Eerys / they be tabourerys, 883
The tenour Round / And mery goo the bellys;
<small>They are worse than briars, the torments of Tantalus, or the flowers of Proserpine.</small> But with ther touch / they stynge wers than brerys,
With hunger, thrust / myd tantalus dyuers wellys,
fflours of proserpina / fayr and bittir smellys: 887
So semblaby / flatererys in Apparence,
Be outward sugryd / And galle in existence. 889

(128)

And he that wyl / be famous in largesse, 890
And haue a name / of liberallyte,
<small>A king should consider the merits of high and low degree.</small> lat hym Conceyve / Aforn in his noblesse,
The discertys / of hih and lowe degre,
Atwen mesour / excesse and skarsete, 894
So departe / by Attemperaunce,
That lyk discertys / Ech man haue Suffysaunce. 896

(129)

In the partyng / stant Wysdam and fooly, 897
but discrecioun / medle in this matere;
<small>He should only reward the worthy.</small> Who yevith his tresour / to them that be wourthy,
And them guerdownyth / with glad face and Cheere,
As Ryght and Resoun / in tyme doth Requeere 901
In his departyng / As to myn Avys,
Suych a kyng / is provident and wys. 903

and be bounteous only to the Worthy. 29

(130)
But whoo departith / his tresour and Rychesse 904 [fol. 22 b.]
 To them that been / not wyse nor profitable,   and not the unwise;
It is Callyd / A maneer of excesse,
 Which in A kyng / is nat honourable.
Of prudent partyng / in Corages that be stable, 908
 Ther folwith Afftir / by Repoort of Wrytyng,
Greet laude and preys / namely in a kyng. 910

(131)
To them that falle / in Casuel indigence, 911 he should help those who fall into undeserved poverty,
 Be sodeyn Caas / Or in necessyte,
Or infortunys / froward violence,
 Than it accordith / to Royal dignite,
To shewe of ffredam / his liberallite : 915
 Suych a kyng / Advertisyng his Charge,
Is to hym Sylff / and to his liges large. 917

(132)
And his lordshippe / And al his Regioun 918
 Shal encrese / in long felicitye,
With laude and preys / love and subieccioun,
 As Appartenyth / vnto his dignite,
To were his Crowne / in long prosperite ; 922
 I dar afferme / and mak my Sylf wol boold,
Suych wer Comendid / of philisoffres Oold. 924

(133)
But yif a kyng / Contraryous of sentence, 925 [fol. 23 a.]
 partith his tresour / to them that ha no nede,
Or be nat falle / in Casuel indigence,
 but wylfully / lyst nat taken hede, but not those who have wasted their goods
What evir he spent / Cast aforn no drede : 929
 This folwith therof / his tresour and his Cost,
With-Oute laude / bothe two ar lost. 931

(134)
Suych Oon gladly / wheer he wake or wynke, 932
 Escapith nat / be vanyte or veynglorye, through vanity or carelessness.
Of poverte / to fallyn in the brynke ;
 The philisoffre / put also in memorye
Suych fooly waast / get On him-Sylf victorye, 936

Things unsuitable to a King.

And Causith hym / be excessyf dispence,
ffolk in daungeer / of froward Indigence. 938

(135)

Description of a prodigal. In his departyng / whoo is inmoderat, 939
This to seyn / whoo is nat mesurable
In his Rychesse / but disordinat,
Is Callyd prodigus / which is nat honourable,
Depopulator / A wastour nat tretable, 943
Which is a name / As be Old wrytyng,
Disconvenyent / to euery wourthy kyng. 945

(136)

[fol. 23 b.] Aristotiles / geyn this Condicioun, 946
Set a Rewle / to Royal providence,
Moost notable / which in Conclusyoun
Shal directe / And Rewle his Clemence
In long prosperyte / of Royal Reuerence, 950
And good Repoort / which is a thyng divyne,
Tressyd as phebus / thorugh al the world to shyne. 952

(137)

Things unbecoming a king. Ther is A maneer / disconvenience 953
In Re publica / is hoolde vicious,
A kyng to pleyne / vpon Indigence,
Outhir in desirs / to been Avaricious,
Outhir skars in kepying / large or Coveytous, 957
Or kepe a meene / twen vertuous plente,
Atwen largesse / and prodigalyte. 959

(138)

It hath be seyn / that Ovir large expence 960
In Regiouns / and many greet Cite,
Hath vnwarly / brought in Indigence,
Bothe in Estatys / And in the Comounte;
Hermogenes' opinion. but hermogenes / of greet Auctoryte, 964
Wroote in A somme / pleynly Concluding
That the noblesse / of a famous King, 966

(139)

[fol. 24 a.] Vndirstondyng / breffly to Conclude, 967
Was perfeccioun / vp lokkyd in sentence,
Signed in a kyng / and the plenitude

Of his Royal / Crownyd magnificence,
And hym Sylff / to have an Abstinence 971
  In his desirs / fro thyng that nat good is,
  ffrom the tresour / and his liges goodys. 973

How Aristotil declarith to kyng Alisaundre of the stoonys.

(140)

TOuchyng the stoon / of philisoffres Old,   974 The philosopher's stone.
  Of which they make / moost souereyn mencioun,
But ther is Oon / as Aristotil toold,
  Which alle excellith / in Comparysoun,
Stoon of stoonys / moost souereyn of Renoun ; 978
  Towchyng the vertu / of this Ryche thyng,
Thus he wroot / to the moost souereyn kyng : 980

(141)

O Alisaundre / grettest of dignite, 981
  Of al this world / monark and Regent,
And of al naciouns / hast the souereynte,
  Echoon to Obeye / And been Obedyent ;
And to Conclude / the ffyn of our Entent, 985
  Al worldly tresour / breeffly shet in Oon,
Is declaryd / in vertu of this stoon. 987

(142)

Thou must first / Conceyven in substaunce, 988 [fol. 24 b.]
  by A maneer / vnkouth divysioun,
Watir from Eyr / by a dysseveraunce,[1]   The elements Water and Fire must be separated from Air,
And ffyr froom Eyr / [2]by a departysoun,[2]
Echoon preservyd / ffrom Corrupcioun, 992
  As philisoffres / Aforn haue Speceffyed,
Which by Resoun / may nat be denyed. 994

(143)

Watir from Eyr / departyd prudently,
  Eyr ffrom ffyr / And ffyr from Erthe doun, 995 and all three carefully purified.
The Craft conceyved / devyded trewly,
  With Outyn Errour / or decepcyoun :
Pure euery Ellement / in his Complexioun, 999
  As it partenyth / pleynly to his part,
As is Remembryd / perfightly in this Art / 1001

---

[1] 'deperte' in MS.   [2–2] blank in MS.

Some great Alchemists.

(144)

The colour of the stone is Citron for gold making,

This stoon of Colour / is Sumtyme Cytrynade   1002
   lyk the sonne / stremyd in his kynde,
Gold tressyd / makith hertys ful glade,
   With moor tresour / than hath the kyng of ynde,
   Of precious stoonys / wrought in ther dew kynde :   1006
     The Citren Colour / for the sonne bryght,

white for silver making.

     Whyte for the moone / that shyneth al the nyght.   1008

(145)

[fol. 25 a.]

Philip of Paris wrote of the purification of the elements.

This philisoffre / brought forth in parys   1009
   Which of this stoonys / wroot fully the nature,
Al the divisyoun / set by greet Avys,
   And ther vpon / did his besy Cure,
   That the perfeccioun / longe shulde endure   1013
     lyk thentent / of Aristotiles sonde,
     Which noon but he / Cowde wel brynge on honde. 1015

(146)

ffor though the matere / Opynly nat toold   1016
   Of this stoonys / what philisoffres mente,
Aristotiles / that was expert and Oold,
   And he of parys / that forth this present sent,
   And in al his beste / feithful trewe entent,   1020
     With circumstaunces / of Arrabye, ynde, and perce,
     Towchyng the stoonys / that Clerkys Can Reherse ; 1022

(147)

Hermogenes was the tutor of Philip,

Hermogines / hadde hym Sylff Alloone,   1023
   With seyd Phelip / that with hym was Secree,
knewh the vertu / of euery prevy stoone,

and taught him all the virtues of stones.

   As they were / dispoosyd of degree,
   ffrom hym was hyd / noon vnkouth previtiee ;   1027
     This hermogenes / and he / knewh euery thyng
     Of alle suych uertues / as longe to a kyng.   1029

[fol. 25 b.] **how kyng Alisaundre must prudently Aforn conceyve in his providence.**

(148)

A king must not run into

TO eschewyn / alle excessys prudently,   1030
   And specially / al froward Outragious largesse,
Avaryce and / gaderyng frowardly,

How a wise King may be known.

Wheer trouthe and ryght / have an enteresse.
ffor he that wastith / and spendith by excesse 1034 *excess of liberality,*
The grete goodys / and pocessyouns,
Wheer he hath lordshippe / and domynaciouns. 1036

(149)
A Rewle groundid / On discrecioun 1037
Geyn Appetites / that be bestial, *or of appetites;*
Oonly Conveyed / And brydlyd by Resoun
To withstande lustys / that be Carnal,
Geyn Avaryce / in Especial; 1041 *especially of avarice,*
ffor Coveitise / with desir of Rychesse,
Doth in a kyng / Avaryce Represse. 1043

(150)[1]
Which Causith first / in his Regalye 1044 *which causes many harmful things.*
Wilful vntrouthe / by fals presumpcioun,
By extort poweer / groundid On Robberye
Geyn goddys lawe / wilful destruccioun
In al his werkys / for short conclusyoun, 1048
To procede / by Recoord of scrypture,
In prosperite / shal nat longe endure. 1050

how witt of Sapience or of discrecioun may be parceyvid in a kyng or a prynce.[2]

(151)
First that the fame / of Royal Sapience, 1051 [fol. 26 a.]
So that Repoort / of his notable ffame
Be voyde of vices / that Cleer intelligence
In his Empyre / be cleer from al diffame,
That no Repoort / blott not his name, 1055 *He bears a good name among his subjects;*
Nor no fals Counsayl / of folkys that be double
The Cleer shyning / of his good name trouble. 1057

(152)
This is to seyn / that he be quiete & peysyble, 1058 *is peaceable,*
Sogettys to kepe / hem from divysioun,
And nat lyghtly / to be Credyble
To talys / that make discencioun.
ffor wheer pees Regnyth / is al perfeccioun. 1062
Kepith sogettys / as they shulde be, *and keeps down internal strife.*
ffroom alle stryves / quiete and vnite. 1064

[1] Omit Sl. 2027.   [2] In margin of MS. PHILOSOPHERS.

how a kyng shuld be Religious.

(153)

<small>He should be merciful, yet just;</small>

A kyng also / shulde been of lyff, 1065
by good exaunple / Sad and Religious,
Merciable / and kepe hym out of stryff,
And in his doomys / nat been to Rygerous,
Chastyse alle / that be vicious, 1069
Namely, alle / that be founde shrewys
And Contrarye / vnto good thewys. 1071

(154)

<small>[fol. 26 b.] and especially put down heretics and enemies of holy church,</small>

Off ful purpoos / hoolly for to werche 1072
To Chastice hem / of Equite and Right,
That been Enmyes / vnto hooly Cherche,
On heretiques / for to preve his myght;
And yif ther be / Ony maner wyght, 1076

<small>and bold lawbreakers.</small>

Hardy in dede / of presumpcioun,
To ffende his lawes / haue dewe Correccioun. 1078

how a kyng shulde be arrayed lych his Estat.

(155)

TO a kynges / Royal mageste, 1079
Array which is / Ryche and honourable,
pertinent / to his dignite,

<small>A king's demeanour and presence.</small>

Sad of his Cheer / in his demenyng stable,
And of his woord / nat feynt nor varyable ; 1083
Also of his behest / trusty and ek trewe,
Sad as a Saphir / and alwey of Oon hewe. 1085

how this vertu Chastite apperteyneth wel in a kyng.

(156)

NOble prince / Considere in thy Estat Royal 1086
how this vertu / Callyd Chastite,
Is a vertu / and in Especial

<small>The evils of lechery in a king.</small>

With abstinence / from al dishoneste ;
And greet Recours / of ffemynynyte 1090
pallith of prynces / the vertuous Corage,
And Or ther tyme / makith hem falle in Age. 1092

how it longith to a kyng oonys in the yeer to shewe hym in his Estat Royal. [fol. 27 a.]

(157)

Afftir the Custom / of Royal excellence, 1093 *The Romans teach that a*
And the vsage / Ek of Rome town, *king should be seen in*
kynges ar wont / in ther magnificence, *full state by*
To shewe ther noblesse / and ther hihe Renoun, *his people,*
Ther lordshippe / and domynacyoun 1097
To kepe ther Sogettys / verrayly in dede,
Vndir a yerde / atwix love and drede. 1099

(158)

So that love / haue a prerogatyff 1100 *to retain*
To be preferryd / Suych as haue poweer *their love and fear.*
To shewe hem Sylff / duryng al ther lyff
Of discrecioun / avoydyng al daungeer ;
This to seyn / ech estat / in his maneer 1104
Shal dewly / with euery Circumstaunce,
As they ar bounde / doon ther Observaunce. 1106

Of his dewe observaunce that longith to a kyng.[1]

(159)

Afftir his lawes / his statutys to Obeye. 1107 *His laws must be*
Peyne of deth / no wyght be Contrarye, *implicitly obeyed,*
What he Comaundeth / his byddyng to with-seye ;
ffor what euere / from his precept varye,
Or On his byddyng / be slouhe or lyst nat tarye, 1111
Ther is no more / vpon that partye
but lyff and deth / stonde in Iupartye. 1113

(160)

Whoo so euere / of presumpcioun, 1114 [fol. 27 b.]
Dar attempte / On ony maner syde *and his rights maintained.*
The kynges Ryght / in his Oppynyoun
To interupte / of malyce or of pryde,
And ther-vpon / presvme tabyde, 1118
To with-stonde / the kynges Royal myght,
Or ony thyng / that longith to his Ryght. 1120

[1] Before (160) in MS.

how solace and disport longith to a kyng.

(161)

He should entertain himself with music and shews.

And that it longith / also to a kyng, 1121
With Instrumentys / of hevenly Armonye,
ffor his dispoort / prynces Abydyng
fful solempnely / with divers menstralcye,
To Recounfoorte / and glade his Regallye 1125
And Comownerys / with entieer dilligence,
With Ryght hool herte / Reioysshe his presence. 1127

What appartenyth also to his glorye.

(162)

He should keep about him a splendid court.

To his noblesse / & his singuler glorye, 1128
To haue aboute hym / many a wourthy knyght
ffor Chevalrye / Conservith the memorye,
And the sonne / alweye to shyne bryght,
That it shal nat / Eclypsen of his lyght; 1132
But thorugh the world / bothe in lengthe & brede,
As ffyry phebus / bothe shyne and sprede. 1134

[fol. 2*r*. a.]
The Similitude of a Kyng.

(163)

IN four thynges / must considred be 1135
Toward god / his Obedience,
And to the peple / his liberallyte
As they disserve / with dewe Reuerence
The kyng taquite / in his magnificence. 1139
As his sogettys / be goodly to hym seyn,
Lyk ther decertys / he quyte so Ageyn. 1141

how a kyng shulde be gouernyd in al maner of wedrys.

(164)

FOr herthe / holsom be the Reynes, 1142
It Causith flours / fresshly for to sprede,
And makith medwys / And Agreable pleynes
To shewe ther bewte / bothe in lengthe and brede
And Ovir moore / Whoo that takith hede, 1146
With Oute moysture / and cherysshyng of the Reyn,
In his bewte / Comyth nouthir / flour nor greyn. 1148

Off hys dewe obseruance
that longyth to a kyng

Whoo ys ond of presumpcion
Day attempte / on ony mans syde
The kynges Ryght / in his opynyon
To interupte / of malyce or of pryde
And thou vpon / presome tabyde
To with stonde / the kynges Royal myght
Or ony thyng / that longyth to his Ryght /
How place and disport / longyth to a kyng

And that it longyth alß to a kyng
With Instrumentys of hevenly armonye
ffor his disport / pryncesse abydyng /
ffull solempnely / with diuerse menstralsye
To recomforte / and glade his Royaltye
And to morowys / with entiere diligence
With Ryght hool herte / worsshipe his presence

What appartenyth / alß to his glorye /

And his noblesse / & his singuler glorye
To have a boute hym many a worthy knyght
ffor the labour / to serveth the memorye
And the same / alwey to shyne bryght
That it shal nat Eclypson / of his lyght
But thorugh the world / bothe in longthe & brede
As ffery phebus / bothe shyne and sprede /

A King should be merciful and faithful.

(165)

By a maneer / Iust Similitude,   1149   *The king's grace should be like the rain of heaven.*
  As Reyn counforteth / eue*r*y Erbe and tree
bra*u*nchys a-loffte / pleynly to conclude,
So shulde a kyng / of his benignite
  Shewe hym gracyous / to hihe and lowe degre,   1153
    That eue*r*y wyght / with dewe Reue*r*ence
  Shulde with glad cheer / parte from his p*r*esence.   1155

how a kyng shuld be m*er*cyable.

(166)

A kyng Also / in his Estat notable,   1156   [fol. 28 b.]
  To his sogettys / of hih and lowh degre,
Shulde be gracious / and merciable,
  love Rancour / and haue on hem pite ;
  preserve mercy / Considre also and se   1160
    That mercy is vertuous / in his Trone,
  Crownyd with gold / moost singuleer allone.   1162

It longith to a kyng specially to kepe his promys.

(167)

A kynges promys / shulde be Iust & stable,   1163
  As a Centre / stonde in O degre,
Nat Chaunge lightly / nor be varyable,
  And be-war / of mutabylite.
  Woord of a kyng / mvt stonde in O degre ;   1167
    What that eue*r*e / that a prynce seith,
  The Conclusyou*n* / dependith vpon feith.   1169

how stodye & clergye shuld be p*r*omotyd in a kyngdome.

(168)

As the sonne / shewith in his guyse   1170
  Mong smale sterrys / wit*h* his bemys bryght,
Ryght so in / the same maner wyse,   *The praise of a University*
  An vniue*r*site / shewith Out his lyght
  In a kyngdom / As it shulde be of ryght,   1174
    And by the prynce / have dewly favour,
  So Clergye beryth / a-wey the fflour /   1176   *and of Clergy.*

38 *The Duties of a King's Leech.*

(169)

[fol. 29 a.] Wheer is Clergye / ther is philosophye, 1177
Clergy promote philosophy and trade. Marchaundyse / plente and Rychesse,
prudent Counsayl / diffence of Chevalrye.
In ech Estat / Wysdam, gentillesse,
Curtesye, ffredam / and prowesse ; 1181
And as the kyng / tencrese his name,
His peple wyl folwe / and gladly duo the same. 1183

how a kyng hovith to haue a leche to kepe his body.[1]

(170)

The king's leech must be a good astronomer For helthe of body / the kyng of hool entent 1184
Must haue lyk / to his desir
Suych Oon / as knoweth the firmament,
And is expert / A good Astronomeer,
Which that knoweth / sesouns of the yeer ; 1188
as Cyprian was, As in his tyme / was Oold Cypryan,
A philisoffre / and an expert man. 1190

(171)

who knew the four qualities, He knewh the Cours / of planetys & disposicioun, 1191
Of moyst and drye / both of heete & Coold,
and all the changes of nature. Chaung of the yeer / And Revolucyoun.
ffor in which thyng / he was expert and boold :
Of the Cours of planetys / manyfoold, 1195
And of Elementys / the Revuluciouns,
Chaung of tymes / and Complexiouns. 1197

(172)

1198
[fol. 29 b.] And specially / in Astronomye
He must point out times for sleeping and waking, knowe the tyme / whan he shal slepe or wake,
vndir a Rewle / of philosophye,
In no wyse / that he noon excesse make.
He mvt also / Al surfeetys ek forsake ; 1202
and restrain the king's appetites. ffor Ony lust / of froward Appetyght,
Counseyl of lechys / to modeffye his delyght. 1204

(173)

1205
The virtues of the planets— Saturn, Mars, the Sun, Mercury, Satourn is Slouhe / mars malencolyous,
And phebus Causith / dysposyng to gladnesse,
In Rethoryk / helpith mercuryvs,

How a good Leech may be chosen. 39

ffor in the moone / is no stabylnesse.
ffortune braydeth / ay On doubylnesse,   1209 *and the Moon.*
And sith a kyng / vpon ech partye
Stant vpon Chaunges / ful hard hem to guye.   1211

how a kyng shuld be gouernyd in Astronomye.

(174)

A Stronomerys / that knowe previtees,   1212 *Astronomy as a means of diagnosis.*
  helthe of body / discrasyng of syknesse,
dyuers Causes / of Infirmytees,
Wherof ffeuerys / doo so greet distresse,
Achys, gowtes / of drynkes greet excesse :   1216
And Out of tyme / be war of long wacchyng,
Which to the helthe / is contrarye to a kyng.   1218

Next folowith the vtilite of the helthe of a kyng.

(175)

O Alisaundre / lych as providence   1219 [fol. 30 a.]
  Of suych as been / expert lechys,   *Trust to doctors proved by experience.*
Suych as been prevyd / by experience,
And prevyd Auctours / as the phesyk techys,
Truste On the dede / And nat in gay spechys ;   1223
Woord is but wynd / leff woord and tak the dede,
Thyng wel expert / disservith wel his mede.   1225

how mechil a-vayl is comprehendid in the diligence of a good leche.

(176)

A good leche / expert in A kyng   1226 *The results of having a good leech.*
  ffor dilligent / Conservaciouns,
A kynges helthe / be wrought in al thyng,
So that in qualyte / be founde noon Erryng
Nor hyndre his Appetyght / in mete nor drynk ;   1230
Nor be discrasyd / to hyndre his Appetyght,
Wherof nature / hath Contraryous delyght.   1232

(177)

And O Rewle / specially shal I the teche,   1233
  Towchyng the tyme / And hour of his dyete,   *The time of eating.*
So he nat wante / the presence of his leche :

        To his Complexioun / as it is moost meete,
        Tyme set Atwen / Coold and heete,   1237
          With this Reward / by Resoun to expresse,
          By good avys / that he doo noon excesse.   1239

[fol. 30 b.]   **A special Epistil to the Singuleer helthe of a prynce.**

(178)

N Aturel philisoffres / assentyd alle in Oon,   1240
    Seyn that a man / is maad of iiij. humours,

None of the four humours of man's body should be in excess.
  And they Assentyn / in wryting euerychoon
  Afftyr the wedyr / Reynes, haylles, and shours,
    planetys a-loffte / and the hevenly tours.   1244
    Afftir they sette / in the hevene a governaunce
  In Erthe folwyth / of helthe Attemperaunce.   1246

(179)

Of mekil excesse / folwyth Corrupcioun,   1247
  Excesse of travaylle / Causith febylnesse.
Thought sorwe / be greet Occasyoun,
  To engendre / greet Syknesse,
  And puttith folk / in froward distresse,   1251
    That vndigestion / with Oute Remedye,
    Causith ofte sithe / by processe that they deye.   1253

To conserve hele aftir a mannys Complexion.

(180)

A fftir drynesse / and humydite,   1254
   And Chaungying also / of Complexiouns,
Of Etyng, drynkyng / wheer as necessyte
  Requeryth his tyme / and yif purgacyouns
  Be necessarye / Afftir the sesouns   1258
    Solve flewm / brennyng or moysture,
    To kepe a mene / A leche mvt doon his Cure.   1260

[fol. 31 a.]   **how a kyng must take keep whan he shal reste and whan he shal sleep.**

(181)

S Leep is noryce / of digestioun,   1261
   Yiff it be take / in attemperaunce,
Yif slogardye / yive Ony occasyoun,

Causith hevynesse / slouthe or disturba*u*nce
Put a man Out / of good governa*u*nce, 1265 Too much sleep is harmful.
Be war of wach / kepe also the date,
To kepe a mesour / of Etyng and drynkyng late. 1267

how a leche shal goue*r*ne a pr*y*nce slepyng & wakyng.

(182)

Y If thou wilt been hool / & kepe þᵉ fro syknesse, 1268
And Resiste / the strook of pestilence,
look thou be glad / and voyde al hevynesse; Rules for good health.
ffteen wykked Eyerys / eschewe the presence
Of enfect placys / Causyng the violence; 1272
drynk good wyn / and holsom metys take,
Walke in Clene Eyr / eschewe mystes blake. 1274

(183)

And yf so be / lechys do the faylle, 1275 Even in the absence of leeches,
Than take good heed / and vse thynges thre,
Temperat dyete / and temperat travaylle,
Nat malencolyous / for noon Adversite,
Meke in al trouble / glad in poverte, 1279
Ryche with litel / content with suffysa*u*nce;
Yif phesyk lakke / make this thy goue*r*na*u*nce. 1281

(184)

Afftir mete be-war / make no long sleep, 1282 [fol. 31 b.]
Heed, foot, and stomak / preserve hem ay fro Coold.
Be nat to pensyf / of thought take no keep,
Affter thy Rente / mayntene thyn housoold;
Suffre in tyme / and in thy ryght be boold, 1286
Swere noon Othys / no man to be-gyle,
ffor worldly Ioye / lastith here but a whyle. 1288

(185)

Thus in two thynges / stondith al welthe 1289 health of body and soul consists in diet and charity.
Of soule and boody / whoo so lyst hem sewe;
Moderat ffoode / yevith to man his helthe,
And al surffetys / doth from hym remewe,
And Charyte / to the sowle is dewe. 1293
Wherfore this dyete / O Alisaundre, kyng!
To alle indifferent / is Rychest thyng. 1295

Spring; its Qualities and Effects.

Of the foure sesouns of ye yeer I gynne at veer.

(186)

Spring described.

What tyme the sesoun / is Comyng of the yeer, 1296
 The hevenly bawme / Ascendyng from the Roote,
The ffresh Sesoun / of lusty grene veer,
Which quyketh Corages / and doth hertys boote,
Whan Rounde buddys / appere on braunchys soote, 1300
The growyng tyme / and the yong sonne;
I mene the sesoun / whan veer is be gonne. 1302

(187)

[fol. 32 a.] And bright phebus / Entryth the Rammys hed, 1303
 And begynneth / Ascendyn in his spere,
Whan the Crowne / of Alceste whyte and Red,
Aurora passyd / ful fresshly doth Appere;
ffor Ioye of which / with hevenly nootys clere, 1307
The bryddys syngen / in ther Armonye,
Salwe that sesoun / with sugryd mellodye. 1309

(188)

The qualities of spring.

Twen hoot and moyst / this veer is temperat, 1310
 Havyng his moysture / of Wyntres sharp shours,
Of somyr folwyng / to fflora consecrat,
Hath moderat heete / be Recoord of Auctours;
The sesoun Ordeyned / taraye with newe Clours, 1314
As gardeyns Erbys / and to sowe seedys,
And the lusty Silvir dewh / in the grene meedys. 1316

(189)

Entryng this sesoun / wyntir doth leve take, 1317
 ffrostys departyd / and molte with the sonne,
And euery ffoul / Chosen hath his make,

The nightingale; the rabbit;

And nytyngalys / for Ioye her song hath be gonne;
Yonge Rabettys / be to ther Claperys Ronne, 1321

the cuckoo.

And the Cokkow / that in Wyntir dare
In euery lay to synge / she lyst nat for to spare. 1323

(190)

[fol. 32 b.] Lovers of Custom / do this sesoun preyse, 1324

The lovers' season.

And yonge folkys / flouryng in tendir Age,
Erly a morwen / Tytan makith hem Aryse;

Spring and Youth : Summer and Manhood. 43

So Can nature / prykke them in ther Corage,
Walkyng by Ryvaylles / holdyng ther passage   1328
On plesaunt hylles / so holsom is the Ayr,
Havyng great Ioye / the wedir is so ffayr.   1330

(191)

Wherfore Alisaundir / whoo so take hede,   1331 The moral drawn.
And lyst consydre / by good Avisement,
Of our yong Age / Accounte we must in dede
How that we hau / dyspendid ou[r] talent,
Outhir lyk foolys / or lyk folkys prudent,   1335
To vs commytted / whyl we haue been here,
To for the Iuge / whan we shal appere.   1337

Next than folowith the sesoun Callid Estas.

(192)¹

NOw veer is past / with al his grene levys,   1338
Aprylle and May / with hire sharp shours,
The silver dewh / in woodys and in grevys,
hath spred his bawme / On bankys & on clours;
And next folwyth Estas / with his somyr flours,   1342 The qualities of summer.
As seith thes clerkys / by discrypcioun,
Is hoot and drye / of Complexioun.   1344

(193)²

This tyme gynneth / soone vpon Barnabe: 1345 [fol. 33 a.]
Iune, Iule, August / lastith this sesoun,   Summer lasts from St. Barnabas till St. Bartholomew.
Endith in Septembre / the sonne in Virgine
Hoot and drye / of disposicyoun,
And Coleryk / of Complexioun,   1349
As is Remembryd / of Auctours Olde,
Endith with Bertylmew / with his dewys colde.   1351

(194)

Ffyr, Colour, Estas / and Juventus Age,   1352 Comparison of Youth and Summer.
To-gidre Accorde / in heete and drynesse,
And Coleryk men / Citryn of visage,   Summer and the choleric humour.
Rough, slyh, and Angry / Sume haue gret hardynesse
Off growing slaundre³ / fumous of hastyness,   1356

---

¹ Omitted in Harl. 4826, 14408, Ar. 59, Sl. 2027, Harl. 2251, Lansd. 285.
² Omitted Ar. 59, Harl. 2251.   ³ slendre in MS.

44   *A Description of Summer.*

    With smoke and ffyr / haue greet Accordaunce,
    ffuryous of Ire / froward of dalyaunce.   1358

        (195)[1]
   In this sesoun / Rypith frut and Corn,   1359
    A tyme ful notable / be Comendacyoun,
   This tyme of yeer / Baptist Iohn was born,
    Petir & Poule / suffryd passyoun,
   And petrys cheynes[2] / wer brooke in prysoun; 1363
The holydays The feeste therof / Callyd lammesse,
in Summer. And the translacyoun of Thomas / martryd in Crystemasse.

        (196)
[fol. 33 b.] Been at mydsoomyr / bryng hoony to ther hyvys, 1366
Summer The lyllyes whyte / Abrood ther levys sprede,
scenery. Beestys pasture / and shade hem vndir levys,
   Ageyn the sonne / gras deyeth in the mede,
   Chapelettys be maad / of Roosys whyte and Rede, 1370
   And euery thyng / drawith to his Rypyng,
   As it faryth be man / in his Age growyng.   1372

        (197)
Summer fruit Strawberyes, Cheryes / in gardeynes men may se 1373
and vege- Benys Rype / and pesecoddys grene,
tables. Ageyn heetys / whan men distempryd be
   ffolkys gadre purslane / and letuse that be Clene.
   This sesoun fflora / that is of fflours quene,   1377
   Hire ffressh motlees / she tournyth now Citryne,
   The vertu of herbys / doth doun ageyn declyne. 1379

        (198)
   In this processe / it nedith not to tarye,   1380
The moral. But Oonly to god / Set thyn Inward entent,
   O Alisaundre / herte and thought nat varye,
   But thank the lord / of what thing / that he sent,
   Povert or Rychesse / ther-with to be content;   1384
   As god disposith / ther in to haue plesaunce,
   As Oon in god / and god thy Suffysaunce.   1386

        (199)
[fol. 34 a.] ffor by the sentence / of Seyntes and of clerkys, 1387
   Of thy discertys / afftir the Rekenyng,

  [1] Omitted in 14408, Ar. 59, Sl. 2027, Harl. 2251, Lansd. 285.
   [2] 'keyes' in MS.

Autumn, its Qualities and Effects.

And lyk the ffrutys / of thy good werkys,
  Thou shalt be guerdownyd / this soth and no lesyng,
With pees Eternal / last at thyn Endyng,   1391   *Each shall receive the fruit of his works.*
  With Cryst to Regne / in the hevenly consistorye,
Whan thou by tryvmphe / hast of thy foon victorye. 1393

Thanne folowith after the Thridde sesoun callid Autumpne.

(200)
This tyme of Custom / set folkys in besynesse.   1394
  Ech tydy man / yevith him to travaylle,   *Harvest time.*
To Repe and mowe / and exclude ydelnesse,
  No man sparyd / and husbondys wyl not faylle
To ryse vp erly / And calle vp the poraylle,   1398
  Blowe ther hornys / or the larke synge,
And Stuff ther grangys / with Corn þt they hom brynge.

(201)
The tyme by processe / voydeth the feeld of greyn,   1401
  Takith awey / from braunchys ther swetnesse,   *Autumn scenery.*
Causeth the trees / of frute to be bareyn,
  The levys falle / the wynd abrood hem dresse,
The day, the nyght / bothe of Oon gretnesse,   1405
  The sonne in libra / Egal be ballaunce,
As is the wyl / of goddys Ordynaunce.   1407

(202)   [fol. 34 b.]
This sesoun is dredfull / and distemperat,   1408
  disposed to feverys / thorugh ayr of pestilence,
Offte Chaungyng / and seeld in Oon estat,   *Autumn is dangerous for sick people.*
  Peryllous for syknesse / and with violence;
Off trouble humours / doth folk ful greet offence,   1412
  ffor flewme this tyme / hath domynacioun;
Be-war of syknesse / that gynneth in that sesoun.   1414

(203)
Erthe, Autumpnus / and Age accordyn in Oon   1415   *Comparison of Autumn and Age.*
  Slough, malencolye / spatlyng euere Among,
Dul Courbyd dounward / whan myght & lust is goon;
  fful of Ire / though he be not strong,
Soone mevyd / wheer it be right or wrong: 1419
  And thus senectus / with Autumpne doth accorde,
He and this sesoun / drawe bothe be O corde.   1421

(204)[1]

Autumpne takith / his leve of seynt Clement, 1422
The tyme dyuerse / and wondir varyable,
With strange passions / sodeynly men schent,
be seknessys / which be unkurable;
And for this sesoun / is unkouth & unstable, 1426
With sodeyn Chaunges / and complexyouns to greve,
Therfore in novembre / he takith his leve. 1428

(205)

Wherfore considre / in thyn Estat Royal, 1429

The moral. Take the moralite / of Autumpne the sesoun,
how it is appropryd / and in Especial
to the thrydde age / and the complexioun
Off the and me / for short conclusyoun. 1433
Wherfore, O Alysaundre / haue in remembraunce,
Peyse euery thyng / and kepe the in good gouernaunce.

[fol. 35 a.] **The fourthe determynacioun of the foure sesouns of the yeer.**

(206)

Afftir hervest / whan men thresshe shevys, 1436
Sowyn whete / gadre wyntre frute in gardynes,
And somyr trees / be bareyn of ther levys,

Winter occu- Men putte in Celerys / Cowche newe wynes;
pations. must lesyth his name / toward seint martynes 1440
muryly drounke / whan it is through ffyn,
And lastith tyl / the sesoun / of Seint Martyn. 1442

(207)

The dayes shorte / the nyghtes wondir longe; 1443
Coold and moyst / of flewme nutrytiff,
Winter Contrary to Estas / the frostys been so stronge.
scenery. In Rootys restith / the vertu vegetatyff,
Grene herbys / and braunchys lost ther lyff. 1447
The sonne this sesoun / beeyng in Aquarye,
beestys to the bynne / for stormys dar not tarye. 1449

(208)

The division Thus the foure sesouns / devided of the yeere, 1450
of the year. ffirst veer whan phebus / doth in his spere aryse,
The growyng tyme / whan buddys oute appere;

[1] Not in MS., but in all others.

A Moralization of the Seasons.

Estas folwyng / whan floures in ther guyse
Sprede on ther stalkys / geyn tytan doth aryse;   1454
Autumpne afftir / which longe doth nat tarye,
And yemps endith / the Ende of ffebruarye.   1456 End of winter.

(209)
Thus four tymes / makith vs a merour Cleer   1457 [fol. 35 b.]
Off mannys lyff / and a ful pleyn ymage.   The moral.
Ver and Iuuentus / togedir haue sogeer,
Estas folwith / longyng to saddere age;
To vs Autumpne / bryngeth his massage   1461
Off Senectus / Wynter last of alle,
How dethys Orlogge / doth On vs calle.[1]   1463

(210)
With veer in youthe / we hadde lustynesse,   1464
Which is inpossyble / ageyn to Recure;
Etas gaff vs strengthe / and hardynesse
fflouryng in ffreshnesse / not longe tendure.
Autumpne afftir / bryngeth vs a ffigure   1468
Off Senectus / Wynter of Crokyd age,
How al thyng passith / halt here no long Ostage.   1470

(211)
Loo Alisaundre / ye mowne se thynges tweyne,   1471
Avauntyng lying / longyng vnto Age;
Malencoly / fals demyng and disdeyne,   Reflections on death.
Many passyouns / Rancour and dotage;
Ende of this lyff / terme of our viage: 1475
ffor decrepitus / hath his marke sett,
This world shal ende / it may nat be lett.   1477

(212)
Thus to make / a Combynacyoun   1478 [fol. 36 a.]
Off veer and youthe / be a manere accordaunce   Comparison of seasons and times of life.
Off mannys sadnesse / and Estas the sesoun
fflouring in lust / tyme of most plesaunce,
Autumpne and eld / with ther greet haboundaunce.   1482
Thanne folwith wyntir / and al doth ovir caste:
So doth age for it / may not alwey laste.   1484

[1] This line and the first six of the next stanza are not in Harl. 2251 or Lansd. 285.

(213)

<small>The last line written by Lydgate.</small>

  Off this forseyd / take the morallite,   1485
   Settith asyde / alle materys spooke in veyn :
  The foure sesouns / shewe in ther degre,
   ffirst veer and Estas / next Autumpne wit*h* his greyn,
  Constreynt of wyntir / wit*h* frostys ovir leyn,   1489
   To our foure Ages / the sesouns wel applyed ;
  deth al consumyth / which may nat be denyed.   1491

here deyed this translator and nobil poete : and the yonge folowere gan his prologe on this wyse.

(214)[1]

<small>Another prologue.</small>

 TEndirnesse of age / and lak of Elloquence,   1492
  this feerful matere / savyng supportacio*un*,
 me hath constreyned / to put in suspence
  ffrom yow, my lord / to whoom Recomendacio*un*
 I mekly do sende / with al Subieccio*un* ;   1496
  The dulnesse of my penne / yow besechyng tenlumyne,
 Which am nat / aqueynted / wit*h* the musys nyne.   1498

(215)

<small>[fol. 36 b.]
Modesty of Benet Burgh.</small>

 Wher flour of knyghthood / the bataylle doth refuse,   1499
  what shulde the dwerff / entre in-to the place ?
 bareyn in sentence / shulde hym Sylf excuse,
  And by presumpcyoun / nat shewe out his fface.
 Off Iohn lydgate / how shulde I the sotyl trace   1503
  ffolwe in secrees / Celestial and dyvyne,

<small>Praise of Lydgate.</small>

 Sith I am nat aqueynted / with the musys nyne ?   1505

(216)

 Ffrenescys sent / from the lady nature   1506
  ffor a conclusyoun / hir Iourne to Conveye,
 As of Anthyclaudyan / Rehersyth the scripture,
  Be sevene Sustrys / in her passage took the weye,
 Gynnyng at grameer / as for lok and Keye,   1510
  In Ordre and proporsyoun / folwyng the doctryne,
 Which was wel aqueynted / wit*h* the musys nyne.   1512

(217)[2]

<small>The seven sciences would blame the Muses if they assisted him.</small>

 These Sevene Sustryn / souereyn and entieere,   1513
  Yif I my penne / to this matere doo applye,
 The nyne musys / blame shal in maneere,

[1] Not in 14408, Ar. 59, Harl. 2251, Lansd. 285.   [2] Not in Lansd. 285.

Pointing out his Unfitness. 49

That they vnlabouryd / stant on my partye.
I yaff noon attendaunce / I may it nat denye. 1517
  how shulde I thanne / my matere doo Combyne,
  Which am nat / aqueynted / with the musys nyne? 1519

(218)[1]

These Sustrys / Cheyned in parfight vnyte, 1520 [fol. 37 a.]
  departe may not / by natural resoun ;   *The sciences are united to each other.*
Ech with othir / hath Eternite.
  how shulde I thanne / vse persuasioun,
Of my purpoos / to haue conclusyoun 1524
  In ech science / fayllyng degre and signe
ffor lak of aqueyntaunce / of the musys nyne? 1526

(219)

Yif I shulde talke / in scyencys tryvyal, 1527 *The trivial sciences;*
  Gynnyng at grameer / in signes and figurys,
Or of metrys / the feet to make equal,   *he knows neither grammar nor prosody,*
  be tyme and proporcioun / kepyng my mesurys,
This lady lyst nat / to parte the tresourys 1531
  Of hire Substaunce / to my Childhood incondigne,
Which am not aqueynted / with the musys nyne. 1533

(220)

This mateer to Conveye / by trewe conclusyoun, 1534
  veritees of logyk / certys I must applye,   *nor logic,*
Wheer vndir flourys / restith the Scorpioun,
  Which I fere / to take for my partye,
Premyssys congrew / which can nat applye, 1538
  Of Old philisoffres / to folwe the Doctryne,
Sith I am nat aqueynted / with the musys nyne. 1540

(221)[2]

I haue with Tully / gadryd no fressh flours, 1541 [fol. 37 b.]
  The Chaar of ffronestis / to paynte in dewe manere, *nor rhetoric of Cicero or Petrarch,*
With Petir petrarke / of Rethoryk no Colours,
  Of teermys ne sentence / in my wrytyng doth appere;
Arismetryk nor musyk / my Dulness doo not Clere. 1545 *nor arithmetic, nor music, nor geometry,*
  how shulde I thanne / by Geometrye drawe ryght lyne,
Which am nat aqueynted / with the musys nyne? 1547

[1] Not in Lansd. 285.   [2] Not in 14408.
PHILOSOPHERS.

nor astronomy of Ptolemy.	(222) Off Astronomye / the Secrees invisible, vnknowe with Tholomye / I faylle cognicio*un*, Which by invencyo*un* / to me be inpossible, With oute Doctours / and exposicio*un* ; Or of this sevene / to make a declaracio*un*, Afftir your entent / this treetys to Combyne, Which am nat aqueynted / wit*h* the musys nyne.	1548 1552 1554
He considers the difficulty of the task, the royal command,	(223)[1] These thynges peysed / myn hand make to quake, Thre Causys / considred in Especial ; ffirst of this book / the difficulte to take, Secunde of the p*e*rsone / the magnificence Royal, To whoom I wryte / in-to tremlyng cause me fal ; Of dirk ignora*u*nce / feryng the Engyne, Which am nat aqueyntyd / with the musys nyne.	1555 1559 1561
[fol. 38 a.] and the detraction of his rivals ;	(224)[1] The thrydde cause / in the Audight co*u*ntable, Entitled and Rollyd / of my remembra*u*nce, Is that detractours / Odyous and detestable, Vnto Allecto / knet be affya*u*nce, With sotyl menys / shal make p*e*rturba*u*nce Affermyng to my witt / to moche that I enclyne The werk to a taste / not knowyng the musys nyne.	1562 1566 1568
and finds himself between Scylla and Charybdis ;	(225) Thus atwen tweyne / p*e*reel of the see, Sylla and karybdys / put in desperacio*un*, What to resceyve / and which for to flee, Constreyned I am / to make dubytacio*un* ; The sharp corosye / of fretyng detraccio*un* ffirst I feere / to my partye shal enclyne, Sith I am nat aqueynted / wit*h* the musys nyne.	1569 1573 1575
	(226)[1] The Secund p*e*reel / by Computacio*un*, In which I stande / this is incertayn ffeer and dreed / of Indignacio*un* Of your lordshipp / which doth nat disdeyn Me to exhorte / to wryte in termys pleyn	1576 1580

[1] Not in 14408, Ar. 59, Harl. 2251, Lansd. 285.

How to keep the Body in good Health. 51

A part of Secrees / Celestial and divyne,
lefft of Iohn lydgate / wel knowyng þe musys nyne. 1582
(227)
Thus set in pereel / fayl I my socour, 1583 [fol. 38 b.]
Me doth counforte / a proverbe in myn entent;   but he is
"Ech tale is endyd / as it hath favour."   comforted by
Wherfore to dreed / no lengere I wyl assent,   a proverb,
but breefly fulfille / your Comaundement 1587 and begins
In modir tounge / this matere to Combyne,   thus:—
Which sauff Support / knowe not the musys nyne. 1589

how a kyng shal conserve natural hete & helthe of body.
(228)
S̃one Alysaundre / of helthe to be sure. 1590
  O thyng I the preye / first and principally   There are
Dewe proporcioun / of heete in nature
To Conserve / for to knowe that Redyly   two causes
In double wyse / man deyeth fynally; 1594 of death,
Off which as by Age / Oon is natural,   natural and
The othir by fortune / As be thynges accidental. 1596 accidental;
(229)
fferthere thy body / to make moyst and fat 1597
Afftir this sentence / folwe my doctryne.
Moche sleep / wyl kepe the / in hih Estat,   how to keep
Metys swete / and wyn licour divyne,   the body in
Merydien Reste / mylk whight and Argentyne, 1601 good health;
Alle good Odours / and flours afftir ther tyme,
With swete bathys / and Erbys good and ffyne. 1603
(230)
Peyse thy tyme / numbre it parfightly, 1604 [fol. 39 a.]
And in the bath / be not Ovir longe,
Tyme contynued / wyl feble the body,
And alle Joyntes / wil weyke / which be stronge;
Drynk no wyn / but watir be ther Amonge, 1608
And iu wyntir / take watir Alchymyn,
Which hot is of nature / to putte in thy wyn. 1610
(231)
The malwe in somyr / And ek violet flours, 1611
Which in nature / be coold of trewthe and ryght,

E 2

To speke pleyn / and vse no Colours,
ffroom Corrupt humours / makith the body light. 1615

a vomit once a month recommended;
Oonys in the monyth / to have a vomyght
purgeth the stomak / makith it pure and clene,
That no Corrupcioun / ther-Inne may be sene. 1617

(232)

fferthere be it knowe / to thy magnificence, 1618
That this vomyght / restoryth hete natural,
Yif it be doo / with oute violence,

its special advantages.
And these Comoditees / Causith in Especial,
Moystnesse good / grees wel to deffye at al 1622
Vndirstandyng / Resoun / glorye and gladnesse,
Of thyn Enmyes victorye / expellith al hevynesse. 1624

(233)

[fol. 39 b.] Yif thou wylt be hool / to kepe the fro Syknesse, 1625
And resyste / the strook of Aduersite,
love to se playes / voyde al hevynesse,
And put delyght / in these thynges thre ;
ffayr men and women / be delectable to the 1629
To be holde / on thy body clene clothyng,
And of Antiquite / to se and rede wrytyng. 1631

Aristotil writ in A pistil to Alisaundre which hurt the body.

(234)

SOne set in a preff / in thy prudent avys, 1632
To ete and drynke / by attemperaunce ;
ffor afftyr the sentence / of philisoffres wys,
The body doon feble / and sette in perturbaunce,
To Ete litel / and drynke with oute gouernaunce, 1636
Sleep before mete / ovir moche travaylle,
With fretyng wratthe / gretly doon disuaylle. 1638

(235)

And who so wyl / breffly in sentence, 1639
Goon ageyn myght / doute or it be nede,
To ech tale / yive hasty credence,

Things harmful to the body.
Offtyn goon to Chaumbir / ovir offtyn to blede,
With salt metys / lyst hym Sylf to fede, 1643
Or drynk Oold Wyn / in greet foysoun,
Doth drye his blood / by natural disposicioun. 1645

The four principal Parts of the Body. 53

(236)
In watir also / Contagious of nature, 1646 [fol. 40 a.]
Be not bathyd / in no degree.
The kynde of brynstoun / is perillous I the sure,   Avoid sul-
And ful replesshyd / I exhorte the   phur baths
    and exercise
fflesshly lustys / and bathis to ffle,   after meals.
  1650
Rennyng afftir mete / and also rydyng,
Which cause wyl / a seknesse / callyd quakyng. 1652

(237)
In Etyng of ffyssh / make no Contynuaunce, 1653
ffor afftir the sentence / of expert Ipocras,
ffyssh / the Complexion / puttith to varyaunce,
And pure blood / Corruptith in short spas,
Medlyd with mylk / Causith boody and fas 1657
With lepre / to be smet / thorugh disposicioun
Off vnkynde humours / by inward Corrupcioun. 1659

how the body is devided into foure principal parties.

(238)
O Alysaundre / peyse in a¹ ballaunce 1660
how principal partyes / foure ther be
In mannys boody / which for Remembraunce
And avayl / to thy magnanymyte
I shal entitle / And yif superfluyte 1664
Of evil humours / to Ony of them enclyne,
I shal the teche / A special medicyne. 1666

(239)
Off this Secrees / to yive the cognicioun, 1667 [fol. 40 b.]
The first membryd / this matere to applye,   The first
Wheer powrys Organycall / vse ther operacioun,   principal part is the
Is the heed / And where in the fourthe partye   head:
Set In resydence / is the ffantasye,
And next in Ordre / ymaginacioun, 1671 the chambers
    of the head;
With mynde / Remembraunce and Estymacioun. 1673

(240)
Yif Superfluyte / or Ony evil humours 1674
Of qualitees gendre / by in-proporcyoun
In the hed / be signes / and Colours,

¹ 'a' not in MS.

signs of
disease in
the head;

knowe thou shalt / the indisposicioun
be this doctryne / and instruccioun :   1678
The Eyen dymme / the browys wex greete,
The noose thrylles shrynke / the templys doon bete.   1680

(241)

remedies for
disease of
the head.

This to Recure / A Souereyn medicyne   1681
  Is Aloes / as sey doctours of ffame,
Soore boylled / in dowset and swet wyn,
  With a Roote / of which is the name
Pulgichyn / which boylle must in same   1685
  Tyl tyme the wyn / half wastyd be,
Which than thus vsyd / is profitable to the.   1687

(242)

[fol. 41 a.] Take these Erbys / souereyn and entieer   1688
  In to thy mouth / with the swete licour,
And them close there / in dewe maneer,
  Which distroye shal / ech Corrupt humour;
And kepe them there / tyl tyme thou savour   1692
  Of amendyng / the Comodite,
And expulcyoun / of Superfluyte.   1694

(243)

Another pro-
fitable thing
for the head.

fferthere to geve / the Enformacioun,   1695
  Of mustard whyte / the seed is profitable
Grounde to poudir / for conservacioun
  Reysed in tyme / a quantite mesurable :
And yif thou be / necligent and vnstable   1699
  In Eyen and brayn / in specially
In these thynges / thou shalt haue gret mallady.   1701

The secund principal part of the body.

(244)

The second
principal part
is the breast.

The secund part / this matere to combyne,   1702
  Is the breest / which yif syknesse
Doo Enfeble / in degre or signe,
  Toknys foure / to the / shal it expresse :

Signs of dis-
ease in the
breast.

Tounge lettyd / mouth salt with bittirnesse   1706
  Or ovir swet / of stomak / the mouth egir,
Ache in membrys / in ech sesoun or wedir.   1708

Disease of the Breast; its Cure. 55

(245)
For the breest thus brosyd / vse this medicyne: 1709 [fol. 41 b.]
 litel to Ete / is good phesyk,
To make vomyth / afftir my doctryne,
 Sugre Roseet / with aloes, mastyk   A remedy.
 Wel Chawyd / as sey doctours awtentyk,   1713
 Reseyved in tyme / *proporcyoun* and mesure,
 Off vnkouth seknesses / the breest doon Recure.   1715

(246)
And yif so be / that these doon the faylle,   1716
 Take Sum Spice / good confortatyff,
Which to the Appetight / gretly doth avaylle,   Another remedy.
 And the body / conserveth in good lyff,
 Causeth pees / where was debat and stryff;   1720
 Alle Corrupt humors / expelleth echoon
 With a letuarye / Callyd Dionysoon.   1722 An electuary.

(247)
In foure wyses / thou shalt have gret peynes   1723
 Yif thou my *counseyl* / refuse in this partye;
Sharp feverys / Ache in heed and Reynes:
 Enpechement / the trewthe to speceffye,[1]   Four evil results of
 *P*ropirly to speke / the tunge which doth denye,   1727 disease in the breast.
 And is Occasyo*u*n / A*u*ctours bere witnesse
 Of many vnkouth / a*n*d stra*u*nge syknesse.   1729

The Thrydde p*r*incipal party of the body.

(248)
The thrydde party / to speke in te*r*mys pleyne,   1730 [fol. 42 a.]
 Is the wombe / in the boody natural,   The third part of the body, the belly.
Which yif evil / in degre or signe conteyne,
 knowe thou mayst / by these thynges in especial:
 Rednesse in the kne / the wombe bolnyth wit*h* al   1734 Signs of disease of the belly.
 Of kynde / causith to goon hevyly,
 Geyn which these medycines / take for Remedy.   1736

(249)
Resceyve inward / sum light purgacio*u*n,   1737 A remedy.
 Which sotil and light / is of nature,

---

[1] This line out in Harl. 4826 and Lansd. 285. Lines 1725 and 6 transposed in MS.

	And of the breest / the confirmacioun,	
	Aforeseid also / wyl it Recure ;	
	And yif thow leve / these medicynes I the sure,	1741
	As Oold philisoffres / Cleerly doon expresse,	
	In many foold / cause it wyl seknesse.	1743

(250)

Evil results of disease in the belly.
 Ache in the Rottle / And Ek in the haunches,   1744
  In bak loyntes / And also Reynes,
With the fflix / And many othir braunches,
Evil digestioun / with othir divers peynes :
This shewith experience / which nevir feynes,   1748
  Modir of konnyng / and cheef maistresse,
  As Oold philisoffres / in wryting ber witnesse.   1750

[fol. 42 b.]   **The fourthe principal parte of the body.**

(251)

The fourth part of the body, the genitals.
 The fourthe party / this matere to combyne,   1751
  Is the genital / founde incerteyn,
Vnto which yif corrupcioun / do enclyne,

Signs of disease in the genitals.
 These be the signes / As philisoffres seyn ;
 Mete to Receyve / the stomak doth disdeyn,   1755
  To Coyllons, yerde / Rednesse doth resoorte,
  Gayn which these medycynes / doon counforte.   1757

(252)

Remedies.
 An Erbe namyd Apus / breffly to expresse,   1758
  With seed of ffenel / is profitable to the,
Off Artemise the Roote / Acheen & Atracies,
Which thus disposed / this seknesse make to ffle :
The herbe the Roote / put togidre al thre,   1762
  With white wyn / drynk it in the morwenyng,
  ffrom seknesse in genital / kepith soget and kyng.   1764

(253)

 fferthere be it knowe / to thy magnificence,   1765
  That watir and wyn / take in smal quantite,
litel to Ete / mesuryd by prudence,

Results of disease in the genitals.
 Among othir / is profitable to the ;
 And yif this doctryne / of the dispysed be,   1769
  Thou shalt Renne / in Ache / of the bladder,
  Which of the stoon / seknesse wyl Engender.   1771

An Ensample how a kyng shulde be inquisitiff to knowe diuers Oppynyouns of lechis or of phisiciens. [fol. 43 a.]

(254)

FErthere I haue Rad / in storyes of Antiquite, 1772
 how to Assemble / made a myghty kyng
Alle phisiciens / hihest of Auctorite
Of Inde and Grece / them streyghtly comaundyng
Oon medicyn to teche / which ageyn al thyng 1776
 Noyows to the body / were Sufficient;
To whoom the Grecys / thus seyde ther entent: 1778

A king desires of learned physicians of India and Greece what is the best medicine.

(255)

"Whoo in helthe / to persevere wyl be sure, 1779
And Conserve / the hete natural
With oute langour / longe to endure,
 hoot watir / to drynke / hym doth be fal:
The mouthe replesshyd / by proporcioun equal 1783
 Tymes thre / in Aurora fastyng,
 Erly to drynke / is moost medicynable thyng." 1785

The Greeks recommend the patient to drink hot water three mornings running.

(256)

The physiciens of ynde / in ther Oppynyoun, 1786
 Seide that madicyne / moost profitable
Was to vse / in dewe proporcioun,
Mylk whyte / with mastursu / thynges medicynable,
Receyved fastyng / moost avayllable 1790
 Man to Conserve / in prosperite and welthe,
 Good inward disposicioun / and bodily helthe. 1792

The Indians recommend him to drink milk and mastursu fasting.

(257)

But knowe Alisaundre / And peyse in ballaunce, 1793 [fol. 43 b.]
 That in this doctryne / myn Oppynyoun
Clerly to entitle / in thy Remembraunce,
 Breefly is this / for ful Conclusyoun,
Whoo slepith wel / be natural resoun, 1797
 Tyl wombe avoyde / al pondorosite,
 Excludyng seknesse / stant in liberte. 1799

Aristotle's opinion.

(258)

Sleep receyved / in tyme and mesure, 1800
 As resoun previth / and experience,
ffroom these seknessys / the boody doth Recure,

The value of seasonable sleep.

Some suitable Meats for Great Men.

  Which previd is / by phisichal prudence.
 Palsy and Gowte / comyng of necligence,   1804
  Ache from the wombe / and Joyntes echoon,
   ffrom tremblyng and quakyng / kepith membir & boon.

(259)

Three good morning medicines. And he that vsith / in morwe these thre thynges, 1807
 Alibi Aurei / thre dragmes in substau̇nce
  Vue passes / or goode and swete Resynges,
  Off flewme warde / shal haue noone perturbau̇nce;
 The mynde hool / excludyng variau̇nce,   1811
  Shal be of kynde / and ygnorau̇nce dysdeyn,
  The boody ffre / from the fevir quarteyn.   1813

(260)

[fol. 44 a.] fferthere to entitle / in the Audight Countable, 1814
 Off thyn Remembrau̇nce / secrees of myn doctryne,
It is good to eat nuts, figs, and rue. Notys te Ete / and fygges is profitable,
 Or levys of Rewe / Agreable and ffyne,
  Geyn al venym / souereyn medicyne;   1818
  And breffly to conclude / in especial
  Alle these conserve / the heete natural.   1820

How profitable is to knowe diuersite & kyndes of metes & drynkes.

(261)

FErthere Alysau̇ndre / be it knowe to the   1821
  That profitable is / in especial to a kyng,
 Of metys & drynkes / knowe dyuersite,
  With proporcioun / and tyme of Receyvyng;
 ffor afftir the sentence / of philosoffres wrytyng, 1825
  Summe are sotil / groos by nature,
  Othir A-twen bothe / in mene kepe mesure.   1827

(262)

Foods which make good blood. Blood pure Engendir / and Enlvmyne   1828
 Metys smale / and sotyl in substau̇nce,
  As whete hennys / Chekenys good and fyne
  The boody norisshe / The stomak kepe fro grevau̇nce;
Those good for labourers are unfit for others. Groos metys / make no perturbau̇nce, 1832
  In labouryng men / which may them deffye;
  In othir / engendir malencolye,   1834

Good Flesh, Fish, and Water. 59

(263)
Which atwen bothe / kepe ther mesure,   1835 [fol. 44 b.]
  As phisciciens / wryte of Auctoryte,
Engendir noon flewm / by kynde of ther nature,
  Ne of humours / superfluite ;
As geet, motown / And othir that be   1839 Hot and moist foods.
  hoot and moyst / in ther operacioun
Moost indifferent / to ech complexioun.   1841

(264)
How be it / that Sumtyme incerteyn   1842
  These flecchys be kynde / make wombe hard & drye,
Yit newly rostyd / Receyved and newly slayn,
  Take fro the speete / and ete hastily,
They be holsom / Resoun doth it not denye :   1846
  And breefly to conclude / this matere in sentence,
Of fysshes the kynde / is lyk thexperience.   1848

(265)
The ffyssh litel / and of sotyl skyn,   1849 The kinds of fish.
  Norysshed in watir / swet and rennyng,
I mene as perche / with the sharp ffyn,   Perch specially mentioned as good.
  be moost holsom / to man them receyvyng :
And in ded watir / bothe Oold and ying   1853
  ffissh norhisshid / is vnprofitable,
And vnto kynde / not avayllable.   1855

The knowyng of watrys, and which be moost profitable. [fol. 45 a.]

(266)
Thow owest to wete / that watir is profitable   1856
  here in herthe / to ech Creature,
To man, woman / and beeste vnresonable,
  Which from Corrupcioun / the body doth recure,
Rennyng from hillys / and erthe which is pure,   1860 Running water is good to drink, where there are no marshes.
  Or neer to Citees / stillyng as perlys Rounde,
Passyng holsom / wher mersshys do noon habounde.   1862

(267)
Watir also / which that is moost lyght,   1863
  Swete or bittir / in ech degree and signe,
ffrom the see / comyng of trewthe and right,
  Thorugh hih hyllys / As perl Argentyne,
knowe may be / whan they be good and ffyne,   1867

7

The six Signs of good Water.

  Be signes sixe / folwyng in sentence,
  Prevyd be resoun / and experience :   1869
    (268)

Different kindes of waters
  Lyght of nature / to make repeticioun,   1870
  Cleer ther-with / and of good Odoure,
  Soone hoot, soone Coold / be dyuers operacioun,
  With oute Corrupcioun / and of good savour,
  White also / and of bright Colour,   1874
  Of which the Contrary / by polityk prudence,
  Thus knowe thou mayst / bexperience.   1876
    (269)

[fol. 45 b.]
which are to be avoided.
  Off slepyng wayours / watrys incertayn,   1877
  Salt, bittir, and fumous / the wombe doon drye,
  In lowe valeys / also which be playn,
  be hoot and hevy / trewthe to speceffye ;
  Wher strengthe of phebus / renewith his partye,   1881
  And watrys ther placys / kepe as they be-gan,
  Of them to drynke / Causeth Coleram nigram.   1883
    (270)

  Watrys that renne / be many diuers londys,   1884
  Be hoot, grevous / vnholsoom, and hevy,
  Which tarage haue / of foreyn dyvers sondys,
  As by experience / previd is redily :

The wrong time to drink water.
  Whoo drynketh watir / ffeblyth his body,   1888
  Afore mete / of stomak heete with-drawith,
  And ful replesshyd / flewme Engendrith.   1890
    (271)

  As Oolde philisoffres / Accoorde al in Oon,   1891
  Sleep is norysshe / of digestion ;

Do not drink water at meal times.
  To drynke watir / as they seye echoon,
  At mete Contynually / causeth Currupcioun
  In the stomak / and is Occasyoun   1895
  Off hevynesse / slouthe and disturbaunce,
  Which puttith a man / out of good gouernaunce.   1897
    (272)

[fol. 46 a.]
Drink cold water in summer,
  Thou owyst to drynke / in somyr watir Coold,   1898
  Namly whan phebus / is in his hih degre ;
  lewk warm in wyntir / in phesyk as it is toold,

The Virtues of Good Wine.

Among othir / is profitable to the:
ffor as doctours / Recoorde of Auctoryte, 1902 and warm in winter.
Coold in wyntir / in euery maneer wyght,
And hoot in somyr / destroye the Appetight. 1904

Of knowynges of vynes, & noynges & bowntes of them.

(273)
SOne Alysaundir / in these secrees devyne, 1905
ffor Chaung of Complexioun / by drynesse or[1] humydite,
Profitable is / in ech degree and signe,
Off wyn to knowe / the werkyng and propirte,
Which receyved / where as necessite 1909
And tyme requeryth / Afftir my doctryne,
Geyn al syknesse / is souereyn medycyne. 1911

(274)
Wyn of the grape / which growith evene vpright, 1912 Hill-grown wine is the best.
Ageyn hillys / to his singuleer counfort,
Where as phebus / with flamyng bemys bright,
Dayly vprisyng / newly doth resoort,
Is moore drye / Afftir philisoffres repoort, 1916
Than othir which / growith naturally
In placys pleyn / moyst and shadwy. 1918

(275)
The first[2] flewmatyk / as folk Oold in age, 1919 [fol. 46 b.]
Gretly doth profite / take by attemperaunce, Whom wine profits.
hoot and yong / puttith to damage,
In Oold mys-humours / restorith to gouernaunce
Superfluytees / and al disturbaunce 1923
Puttith to flyght / and shewith to exigent,
by cause it is / to there nature convenient. 1925

(276)
Wyn moost Reed / and thikke be kynde, 1926 Red and thick wine engenders good blood.
Engendrith good blood / as Auctours repoort,
Which strong and myghty / dullith the mynde,
Take out of mesure / doth not counforte; Its ill effects if taken to excess.
Corrupt humours / causith to Resoorte, 1930
To ech membir / breffly to expresse,
Noyeth the stomak / reyseth wyndynesse. 1932

[1] 'of' in MS.   [2] to' inserted in other MSS.

(277)

  To ech complexio*u*n / of mannys nature,   1933
  Moost medicynable / and lycour indifferent,
Where good wine is grown. Is of the grape / which growith I the sure,
  In large feeldys / to them convenient,   1937
  Strecchyd abroad / with oute inpediment,
  With hillys and valys / Envirownyd aboute,
  Gadryd in tyme / best lycour with outyn doute.   1939

(278)

[fol. 47 *a*.] Breeffly as thus / to exp*re*sse what I mene,   1940
A good grape for making wine. looke they be rype / and of good swetnesse,
  Strong in substa*u*nce / no grenness let be sene,
  ffrom the stok / excludid al moystnesse;
  And of this doctryne / to haue more redynesse,   1944
  looke of wyn of the grape / a litel departyd be
  ffroom the kernel / for lak of humydite.   1946

(279)

The colour of good wine; Wyn holsom also / owith to be of Colour,   1947
  So atwen Red / and gold ffyne,
  Ponya*u*nt, delectable / sharp in savour,
  Thykke at the botme / of Colour Citrine,
  Above Cleer / with licour divine;   1951
  Receyved in tyme / and mesurably,
  Excludyng disese / Co*u*nfortith the body.   1953

(280)

  fferthere Alisaundre / to exp*re*sse what I mene,   1954
  knowe and entitle / in thy Remembra*u*nce,
14 properties of good wine. That wyn good p*ro*pirtees / hath ffortene,
  Off Old philisoffres / peysed in balla*u*nce;
  Enforsyng the stomak / excludith p*er*turba*u*nce,   1958
  ffortefieth the heete / in the body natural,
  Good digestio*u*n / causith in especial,   1960

(281)

[fol. 47 *b*.] Conservith the stomak / from Corrupcio*u*n;   1961
  By al the membrys / the mete doth lede,
  Which convertyd / by transmutacio*u*n,
  Cha*u*ngid to norsshyng / the body doon fede
  With pure blood / of this mat*er*e take hede,   1965

The fourteen Properties of Good Wine. 63

Makith to aryse / the heete be mesure,
ffroom the stomak / to the brayn by nature :   1967

(282)

Evyl humours destroyeth / the Colour makith reed,   1968
Counfortith corages / Clarifieth the sight,
The tounge Elloquent / And delyuer in the heed,
ffroom fretyng malencolye / makith the body light,
Causith good Appetight / makith hardy to fight;   1972
but these be vndirstande / breefly I the sure,
Of wyn receyved / in tyme and mesure.   1974

(283)

And knowe Alisaundre / that wyn Outragiously,   1975 *Too much of it brings about exactly contrary effects.*
Out of tyme / Resceyved, and mesure,
Of these comoditees / Cause contrary,
And the body / longe to Endure,
Doon not permitte / in good Chaung and mesure,   1979
but moo of syknessys / Causith haboundaunce,
That wyn mesuryd / commoditees in substaunce.   1981

(284)

Bookys also / of phesyk and medicynes,   1982 [fol. 48 a.]
be a maneer / of Comparysoun,   *Comparison between wine and rhubarb.*
Atween the Rembarbe / good and holsom Wynes,
This lyknesse / make in disposicioun,
As the rembarbe / holsom of condicioun,
Take out of mesure / is dedly and venym,   1986
ffor short conclusyoun / so holsom is wyn.   1988

Here specially preyseth wyn, and techith a medycyn ageyn drounkenesse of it.[1]

(285)

IN sentence breef / to wryte in termys pleyn,   1989
  Sorippys bittyr / be profitable to the,   *Of syrups.*
fful or fastyng / receyved incerteyn,
Of humours or flewm / whan superfluite
Doon habounde / in signe or degre,   1993
Which in the body / cause Corrupcioun
Of qualitees / shulde be in proporcioun.   1995

[1] In margin of MS.

7 *

Be moderate in Food and Drink.

(286)

The foolishness of those who neglect the help of wheaten bread, good flesh, and good wine;

ffertherre I mervaylle / in myn Oppynyoun, 1996
How man compiled / and maad of foure humours,
May be secke / or tende to Corrupcioun
Whyl he may haue / special thre socours,
Good breed of whete / fflesh that wel savours, 2000
Of tarrage / and stok / good and holsom wyne,
Rcyceyved in mesure / lycour moost divyne. 2002

(287)

[fol. 48 b.]

or who take too much food, too much work, or too much drink.

Contrarye be / of nature to these thre, 2003
Moche to Ete / Ovir moche travaylle,
drynk to Receyve / in superfluite,
Of the body / ech membre doth disvaylle ;
but yif these / the body doon assaylle, 2007
And of drynk / superfluite specially,
be sotyl meenys / vse this remedy. 2009

(288)

A cure for drunkenness.

ffirst to be washid / is profitable thyng, 2010
In watir boylled / hoot and temperat ;
Afftir, ovir / a ryveer rennyng,
To be set / Arrayed to thyn estat,
With salwys, wyllwys / Envyronnd preperat, 2014
Afftir the stomak / anoynted with-al,
With the Onyment / callyd Sandal. 2016

(289)

Phesciciens also / preve be prudence, 2017
How norisshyng / that tyme is the savour,
To nature of / good spices and encence,
Mesuryd in tyme / by dilligent labour ;

Do not leave off drinking suddenly.

And whoo of wyn / lyst to leve socour, 2021
Hym behovith / by Successioun redily
It to leve / and not Sodeynly. 2023

[fol. 49 a.]

Of the Rightwisnesse of a Kyng and of his Counseil.[1]

(290)

FErthere / Alysaundre / gyff Advertence, 2024
 though of accoord / philisoffres expresse,
To a pryncess / hih magnificence.

The duty of a king to his subjects.

Thyng Celestial / is Rightwysnesse,

[1] In margin of MS.

Maad to conserve / the blood and Richesse 2028
Of his sogettys / possessyo*u*ns and werkys,
In which / his Regalye stant / as sey clerkys. 2030

(291)
ffroom god sent / for his Creaturys 2031
Ryghtwysnesse namyd / shap of intelligence,   *Righteousness.*
In sogettys obeysa*u*nt / Souereyn recurys,
Which doth cause / groundid on prudence,
Sent was / noote this sentence, 2035
Vnto pryncee / to conserve froom pillage,
Alle sogettys / extorcio*u*ns and damage. 2037

(292)
Men of ynde / in ther Oppynyo*u*n 2038 *The Indian opinion of a king's duties,*
ffor this concludid / wrytyng berith witnesse,
Off a prynce / for breef conclusyo*u*n,
To his sogettys / bettir is rightwysnesse
Than Abounda*u*nce / or plente of Richesse 2042
In the Reem / and moore Avayllable
Than Reyn froom hevene / A kyng resonable. 2044

(293)
And for they shulde / make no dysseverau*n*ce, 2045 [fol. 49 *b*.]
but ther kyng / And ryghtwysness Ioye in Oon,
Atwen hem / they made Affyau*n*ce, *and how they made a contract with their kings.*
Which was thus wryte / in marbyl stoon :
With oute ryghtwysnesse / prynce may be noon, 2049
And breefly to wryte / with-oute super*f*luyte,
Ryght and the Kyng / as brethryn owen to be. 2051

(294)
It is to the / also greet avaylle, 2052
And accordyng / to thy magnificence,
Oppynyo*u*ns to here / of thy co*u*nsaylle, *How a king should behave in his council,*
And benygly / to gyff audience,
To ther co*u*nsayl / giff advertence, 2056
Intitle and rolle / ech Oppynyo*u*n,
In thy remembra*u*nce / but lerne this conclusyo*u*n. 2058

(295)
Thyn entent / do nat expresse, 2059 *and not allow his own opinion to be known till after.*
Which thou hast / at the begynnyng,
ffor thou owyst / of verray ryghtwysnesse
PHILOSOPHERS.

The Weaver's Son, born to be wise.

	Therof be blamyd / as witnessith wrytyng.	
	keep tounge in mewe / be cloos in werkyng,	2063
	Tyl tyme thou be / in purpoos for avayl,	
	In effect to folwe / ther counsayl.	2065
	(296)	
[fol. 50 a.]	Conceyve the Counseyl / peyse it in ballaunce	2066
Slow in deliberation,	Off eche persone / hih or lowe degre,	
	Which doth Iuge / with oute varyaunce,	
	ffor moost love / which he hath to the ;	
	And whan alle thynges / determyned be	2070
rapid in action.	By thy counsayl / them put to execucioun,	
	ffor to a Reem / delayes Cause destruccyoun.	2072
	(297)	
Delay is dangerous.	To make dellayes / namely tyme of nede,	2073
	Is greet pereel / as philisoffres devyse	
	Off tendir in Age / to this mateer tak hede :	
	Prudent counsayl / loke thou nat despice,	
	ffor sinne of nature / be provident and wyse.	2077
	Summe folkys / by disposicioun	
	Afftir ther tyme / And constellacioun.	2079
	(298)	
	This to conclude / wrytyng I ffynde,	2080
A story of a child born in India	A lyknesse previd / by experience	
	Off an Enfaunt / in the Cuntre of ynde,	
	Boore in a place / where men of intelligence	
	Herborwed were / which gevyng Aduertence	2084
	Of this Child / to ech proporcioun	
	This doom gaff / by natural resoun.	2086
	(299)	
[fol. 50 b.]	Boore he was / vndir such signe,	2087
under fortunate constellations,	Constellacioun / and planete delectable,	
	That he shulde / Enclyne to doctryne,	
	be light of membrys / Curteys and Amyable,	
	lovyd of statys / to Counsayl avayllable,	2091
	Of Sevene sciencys / hauyng in sight cleer,	
son of a weaver,	Whoos ffadir of wevyng / was an Artificeer.	2093
	(300)	
	Tyme passyd / this child grew to Age,	2094
	Weel proporciownyd in membrys Organycalle,	

The King's Son, born to be a Smith.

Whoom his ffadir / for worldly avauntage,
Boonde and dysposyd / to crafft mechanycalle:
but this Enfaunt / for no thyng myght be falle,   2098
  lerne myght / ne for Correccioun,   *who would learn no*
  Be-cause it was / ageyn disposicioun.   2100 *handicraft,*

(301)

They took awey / the brydel of A-reest,   2101 *but, left to himself,*
Hym puttyng / to folwe his owne entent,   *sought company of the*
He sett his herte / to byde with the wyseest   *wisest,*
Of that Cuntre / And moost prudent,
Which in labour / wolde be dilligent   2105
  Hym to Enforme / in science by lecture,
  The kynde of thynges / Conteyned vndir nature.   2107

(302)

The mevyng of the firmament / and al othir thynges   2108 [fol. 51 a.]
vndir nature / he lernyd Redily,   *and learnt all knowledge,*
Good manerys also / to governaunce of kynges,
And by his wysdam / and sciencys fynally,
Be-cause he was / trustyd Specially,   2112 *and became chief of*
  He had the rewle / and disposicioun   *the king's council.*
  Of the kyng / and al his Regioun.   2114

(303)

Contrary to this / in wryting I ffynde   2115
How a nobil / and a Royal kyng
Two Children hadde / in the lond of ynde,
Off which whan Oon / Cam to growyng,   *But there*
He was set / to liberal konnyng,   2119 *was a king's son*
  Taught by mastres / of hih Auctorite,
  As a-partenyd / to his dignite.   2121

(304)

But in that part / he was vntretable,   2122
Maystre ne ffadir / myght no thyng avaylle,
Science nor Crafft / to hym was delectable,   *who would*
but to forge / malyable mataylle: *learn nothing but how to*
Put no delight / in countirfet Apparaylle,   2126 *forge metal.*
  but dysposed / in yong and tendir Age,
  As Child bore / of vile and smal lynage.   2128

F 2

Value Men for themselves alone.

(305)

[fol. 51 b.] The kyng stonyd / greetly in thys partye, 2129
The king, deeply grieved, called together his wise men,
    Of his Reem / Assemblyd in presence
    Alle grettest clerkys / Comaundyng streyghtlye
    That they shulde doo / ther entieer dilligence
    Hym to Enfoorme / by ther science 2133
      Why his sone / of his disposicioun,
      Sauf oonly to forge / wolde take noon informacioun. 2135

(306)

who said that the stars had so ordered it at his birth.
    In ther Oppynyoun / they accoordid alle in Oon, 2136
    And yove this Answere / for ful conclusyoun
    Of his nature / what Enfaunt that wer boorn
      In that signe / or Constellacioun :
      He shulde be / of natural resoun, 2140
        dysposyd that Crafft / Oonly to vse,
        And alle othir / vttirly refuse. 2142

(307)

So that kings ought not to despise wise men of low estate.
    These experymentys / Owe to meve a kyng, 2143
    Nat to despise / A man I the sure,
    litel of stede / and litel of growyng,
    But afftir he spryngeth / in vertu and norture,
    So hym to Cherysshe / owylle of nature, 2147
      Whethir he be / of hih or lowe degree,
      A kyng florysshyng / in excellent dignitee. 2149

(308)

[fol. 52 a.] He owyth to be lovyd / that vices will eschewe, 2150
Whose advice is to be trusted.
    Which lovith trowthe / and counseyllith trewly,
    To the thy sogettys / stedfast, Iust, and trewe,
    And of thy wyl / Sumtyme the contrary,
    Which doth nat spare / to telle the feithfully, 2154
      To this counsayl / yive Affyaunce,
      Which in thy Reem / Cause wyl good governaunce. 2156

(309)

Advice as to government.
    Ordre thy mateerys / afftir ther substaunce 2157
    Set nat the last / there the first shulde be,
    In al nedys / with dewe Circumstaunce,
      To vse consayl / is profitable to the,
      With prevy counceyllours / prudent and secre : 2161

A Father's Counsel to his Son.

ffor good counseyl / moore doth avaylle
Than of pepil / greet puissaunce in bataylle.   2163

(310)
ffor this entent / in wrytyng as I Rede,   2164
A greet man wys / and provident,
Whoos dwellyng / was in the Reem of mede,   *A great man's advice to his son.*
A lettere wroot / and to his sone it sent,
Of which the tenour / and the content,   2168
With the prohemye / and conclusyoun,
This was with oute / varyacioun.   2170

(311)
"Dere sone, it is nede / in al thy werkys   2171 [fol. 52 b.]
To have counsayl / for thou art but O man
Of qualitees contrarye / Compiled as sey clerkys;
Wherfore thy counseyl / take of hem that Can
The directe / by polityk wysdam,   2175 *Two heads are better than one.*
In ech mevyng / habite or passyoun,
The to reduce / by good discrecyoun."   2177

(312)
From thyn Enemy / I counseyl the be sure;   2178 *How to treat enemies, weak and strong.*
Shewe thy poweer / And thyn victorye
Vpon hym / thy ryght to Recure:
But I the monysshe / first and pryncipally,
ffroom hym to tle / in tyme prudently.   2182
Put not confidence / in the greetnesse
Of thyn prerogatyf / and excellent hihnesse.   2184

(313)
Tak counseyl / in thought do not muse   2185
As it plesith / So it Receyve,
The best Accepte / badde do¹ refuse,   *How to take counsel.*
hoo folwith thy wyl / the shal disceyve;
Wers smyt flateryng / than polex or gleyve.   2189
Werfore perceyve / by logical resoun,
Whan vndir flours / restith the scorpioun.   2191

(314)
Be sad of cheer / pley nat the Enfaunt,   2192 [fol. 53 a.]
In answere prudent / wys nat chaungable,   *Do not trust your power into one man's hands.*
Oon singuler man / to make thy leyf tenaunt,

¹ 'not' in some MSS.

How to test your Officers.

  To the ne thyne / is not a-vayllable;
  ffor yif he be wood / and vntretable,   2196
   He may in his / furyous Cruelte
   Thy pepil, thy Reem / destroye, and also the.   2198

(315)

  fferthermore, sone / tak hed to my doctryne,   2199
  To haue officers / is profitable to the,
   Thy worshippe and profight / for to mayntyne:
   And yif thou wylt / lerne this of me,

How to test your officers; Preve thyn officeer / of hihe or lowe degre,   2203
  By sotyl meenys / vse persuasyoun,
  And thanne fynally / take this conclusyoun: 2205

(316)

  Make compleynt / shewe greet hevynesse,   2206
pretend to be in need: ffeyne the nedy / take hym to the neer
  By sotil meenys / thy consceyt to expresse,
   As to thy freend / touche thyn officeer,
   And yif he counseyl / to chevyssh sylveer   2210
    Of thy Iowellys / or thyn tresours,
    he is trewe / and louyth thyn honours.   2212

(317)

[fol. 53 b.] Yif he Caste / or gynne to counte thy dettys,   2213
if he counts up your debts, It is signe / of greet providence;
  ffals and vntrewe / yif of thy sogettys,
   Goodys to Resceyve / he gif Aduertence;
or offers part of his own wealth, And yif he offre / of polityk prudence,   2217
   Part of Richessys / get in thy seruyse,
he is excellent, he is so trewe / no good man may hym mempryse.   2219

(318)

and to be much praised, Comende that Officeer / in thyn Oppynyoun,   2220
  As hym that loueth / moore prosperite,
   Vnyversal / of thy Regioun
   Than pryvat avayl / to his singularyte;
   Signe of good sogett / take this Auctoryte,   2224
as also an officer who is zealous. Is whan he dothe / for thy hih honour,
    Moore than his charge / to thy singuleer plesour.   2226

(319)

  And trust not / On hym of discrecioun,   2227
  Which in tresour / puttith his delight,

The Virtues of a good Officer.

With herte mynde / hath delectacioun,   *Do not trust a covetous man,*
  Good to gadre / Whethir it be wrong or right,
  On whoom growith / evir the Appetight   2231
    In greet Rychesse / And mony to Abounde,
    Which as a depnesse / is with oute grounde.   2233

(320)

Gyff no credence / to such an Officeer   2234 [fol. 54 a.]
  That is Corruptyd / in his affecyoun,   *or one who can be bribed.*
ffor he wyl redily / Seeke mateer,
  And soone consente / to thyn destruccioun:
  Tretyng with lordys / ne cognicioun   2238
    lete hym noon have / and yif he thus offende,
    Oute of thy presence / hym vttirly suspende.   2240

(321)

Love that officeer / of hool herte and entieer,   2241
  Which the lovith / and is ay tretable
To thy sogettys / tak hede of this mateer
  Them to make / to the Agreable,
  ffroom thy seruice / which is not permutable;   2245
    In whoom also / these vertues may be sene   *The fifteen virtues of a good officer.*
    By computacioun / folwyng here ffyftene.   2247

(322)

In membrys parfight / wel to travayllé   2248
  In the Office / hym commyttyd twoo,
Swyfft / vndirstandyng / gretly doth avaylle,
  with redy consceyt / wheer meen haue to doo
That hym is Charged / to execucioun alsoo   2252
    Soone to putte / Curteys and doughty,
    ffayr spekere / with-oute fflattery: 2254

(323)

Groundid in science / and a good Clerk,   2255 [fol. 54 b.]
  Trewe of behest / hatyng lesynges,
gentyl of condiciouns / tretable in ech werk;
  Wel mesuryd / specially in twoo thynges,   *Gluttony is detestable in a king's servant,*
  Mete and drynk / for a-boute kynges   2259
    In-sacyable glotonye / is detestable,
    Inconvenient / and abhomynable.   2261

(324)

	That he¹ love worshepe / and encrese,	2262
	Above al thynges / to thy goodlyheede,
	To gadre gold / leve besynesse,
	ffor as a-fore rehersyd / thou mayst rede
and avarice.	Suych an Officeer / in tyme of nede	2266
	Wyl be enclyned / be persuacio*u*n
	The to destroye / for Ambicio*u*n.	2268

(325)

That he love the / prevy and estra*u*nge,   2269
A good officer loves wise men.   Men of worshepe / put to reu*e*rence,
Which for ²Corrupt[i]on / trewthe wyl not cha*u*nge;
But to ech / be polityk prudence,
Gra*u*nte his labour / and his dilligence   2273
To socoure them / which grevyd be in dispence,
With-oute carnalyte / makyng no difference.   2275

(326)

[fol. 55 a.] In his purpoos / strong and perseuera*u*nt,   2276
His bearing towards others.   With outyn dreed / to se thyn Avaylle,
Meke of condicio*u*ns / and no tyra*u*nt,
Off thyn Rentys / knowyn the Resaylle,
Secreet in werkyng / sharp in travaylle,   2280
ffroom greet spekyng / hym kepith discretly,
ffor moche spekyng / is signe of ffoly.   2282

(327)

In mooche laughtir / that he nat abo*u*nde,   2283
To thy sogettys / gracious and benigne,
Off repoort / ay that he be fo*u*nde,
Trewe and stable / in ech degre and signe
Among the peple / trewthe to mayntene;   2287
To symple also / geve supportacio*u*n,
And them correcte / which vse extorcio*u*n.   2289

(328)

It is to be titled / how prevy with oute obstacle,   2290
As Oold philisoffres / put in Remembra*u*nce,
Man is called the microcosm.   That in man / is founde greet myracle,
Namyd the litel world / by Aucto*u*rs allegea*u*nce,
ffor many and / vnkouth circumsta*u*nce   2294

---

¹ 'He that' in MS.   ² 'Corrupt / on trewthe' MS.

The Properties of Beasts found in Man. 73

ffounde in hym / moost souereyn creature,
Namyd beeste resonable / be intelligence insure.   2296

(329)

He is hardy as leown / dreedful as the hare,   2297 [fol. 55 b.]
  large as a Cok / and as a hound Coveytous,
hardy as an hert / in forest which doth fare,
  Boxsom as the turtyl / As lyownesse dispitous,
Symple as the lamb / lyk the ffox malicious;   2301
  Swyfft as the Roo / as beere slough in taryiug,
And lyk the Ellefaunt / precious in ech thyng.   2303

The twenty-three different animals whose nature is in man.

(330)

As the Asse vyle / and Contagious,   2304
  As a litel kyng / hasty and Rebeel,
Chaast as an Aungel / As swyn leccherous[1],
  Meeke as a pecook / as boole wood and feel;
Profitable as the Bee / in his heve, which is his Cel,   2308
  ffair as the hors / As the howle malicious,
Dowmbe as the ffyssh / And as a mows noyous.   2310

(331)

Noote this processe / in the Audith Countable,   2311
  Of thy Remembraunce / and knowe redyly,
That in beeste / nor thyng vegitable,
  No thyng may be / vnyuersally
But yif it be / founde naturally   2315
  In mannys nature / Wherfore of Oon Accoord
Oold philisoffres / Callyd hym the litel woord.[2]   2317

The title microcosm justified.

Of a kynges Secretary.

[fol. 56 a.]

(332)

FErthere / Alysaundre / Conceyve in thyn entent   2318
  Thy prevy wyse men / for to vndirstande
In speche fair / in language prudent;
  Gay in endityng / fair wryters with hande
looke they be / and ferthere in thy lande;   2322
  looke thy wryters / of thy secrees
In prevy place / wysely kepe thy lettrees.   2324

The qualities of a secretary.

---

[1] Blank in MS.   [2] 'worlde' in all other MSS.

(333)

Lyke as a Robe / fayr[1] of greet Rychesse,	2325
Worshippeth the body / of a myghty kyng,	

How fair language benutifieth a king's letters.

So fair language / trewthe to expresse,	
Worshippeth a lettir / with good endityng;	
look thy secretary / Conceyve in ech thyng	2329
Thyn entent / and it redily	
To execucioun / Can put wittily.	2331

(334)

Thy hihnesse also / for to enhaunce, 2332
And thy magnificence / lerne this of me;

How they should be rewarded.

With greet rewardys / doo them avaunce
Afftir here merytis[2] / and ther degre,
Which aldayes / besy and wakyng be 2336
In thy nedys / for in them stant the warysoun
Of thy worshepe / thy lyf or thy destruccioun. 2338

[fol. 56 b.]

What a kynges massageer oughte to bee.

(335)

FErthere Alysaundre / to spede thy mateerys 2339
ffor a-vayl / Enforce thy Corage

The importance of good messengers,

ffor to haue / swyfft massageerys,
Wys, redy / expert in language,
Moost Sufficient / for thyn Avauntage; 2343

who are the eyes, ears, and tongues of their lord.

ffor a massageer / As philisoffres recoord,
Is the Eye, the Ere / and tounge of his loord. 2345

(336)

His Iourne lette / which lyst for reyn ne shour, 2346
To whoom thou mayst / thy wyl also vncure,
Which the louyth / and thyn honour,
And if thou ne may / of suych Oon be sewre,
At the leste / gentil and demewre 2350

Who should be chosen.

look he be / which wel and feithfully
Can bere a lettre / and repoorte trewly. 2352

(337)

Rakyl of tounge / or moche which doth muse 2353
To gete gifftys / what tyme he is sent

Who are not to be chosen on any account.

On thy massage / hym vttirly reffuse;

---

[1] A blank in MS. [2] 'demerytis' in MS.

And ferthermore / nevir vttir thyn entent
To hym which wyl be Impotent 2357
In al membrys / be Outragious dro*u*nknesse,
ffor more than he knowith / suych Oon wyl ex*pres*se. 2359

(338)
fferthere be prudence / entitle[1] this mateer, 2360 [fol. 57 *a.*]
And it Rolle / in thyn Co*u*ntable mynde,
That hih*e* Estat / ne greet Officeer,   Send no great
On thy massage / thou vse for to sende,   man on your errands,
ffor yif he / to treso*u*n condiscende, 2364 for fear of treason.
Off the and thy Reem / he may be destruccio*u*n,
Whoos punysshment / I remytte to thy discrecio*u*n. 2366

Of Equiperacio*u*n of Sogettys and Con*ser*vacio*u*n of Justice.[2]

(339)
COnceyve dere sone / how the hous of thy mynde, 2367
  be thy sogettys / and the tresour,
By which thy Reem / Confermyd as I ffynde,   How a realm profits by the justice of a king
Doth Contvne / in greet and hih*e* honour,
lyk a gardeyn / of Redolent savour, 2371
Abo*u*ndyng in trees / and divers ffrutys,
Which gryffyd on stokkys / haue many bra*u*nchys. 2373

(340)
The bra*u*nchis sprede / the frute doth multiplye, 2374
And in Caas / lyk and comparable,
Off poweer excellent / trewthe to speceffye,
And of a Reem / tresour perdurable,
By the prudence / famous and agreable, 2378
Off the Comownys / by polityk livyng,
Growe alle vertues / to worshepe of a kyng. 2380

(341)
In werk and woord / and al ther dedys, 2381 [fol. 57 *b.*]
To be mesuryd / is Covennable,
ffroom velonye / and wrong in al ther nedys,
Them to diffende / to the is portable,   who defends them,
Pepil to governe / to the is avayllable, 2385 and governs according to custom.
Afftir Custom / And Condicio*u*n,
In ther partye / vsyd of thy Regio*u*n. 2387

[1] 'eititle' in MS.   [2] In margin of MS.

(342)

<small>Choose good subordinates,</small>

To ther Suppoort / gif them an Officeer, 2388
Which tendith not / to ther destruccioun,
Good of condicioun / wys in ech mateer,
In tyme pacient / vse noon extorcioun
ffor to take this / for ful conclusyoun, 2392

<small>or else fear rebellion.</small>

Yif the Contrarye / thou doo / that I the telle, 2394
Ageyn the / thy sogettys / shul rebelle.

(343)

To encrees of thy Court / And also of thy Reem, 2395

<small>Have impartial judges,</small>

have Iuges trewe / good and wyse,
not parcial / but indifferent men,
Which for lukyr / trewthe will not despyse,

<small>and Courts of Appeal.</small>

Prenotaryes / to haue / I the Advyse: 2399
ne that the Iuges / Corrupt of entent,
Ageyn Iustice / gyf the Iugement. 2401

[fol. 58 a.]

Of the governaunce of Bataylle.[1]

(344)

FErthere Alysaundre / be-hold for thyn avayl, 2402
That to thyn hihenesse / it is Conuenient,

<small>Do not fight in person.</small>

Not to contvne / werre and bataylle;
In thy persone / Conceyve myn entent,
ffor Coveitise or envye / to make busshement, 2406
Or foly to fight / for presumptuousnesse,
Is thyng temerarye / and noon manlynesse. 2408

(345)

Off thy Court / look thou be dilligent, 2409

<small>Find out the popular opinion of men;</small>

ffor to here / the Comoun Oppinyoun,
Thy men of Armys / dispreyse not of entent;
But of me / lerne this conclusyoun,

<small>encourage your soldiers;</small>

Gyf them fair speche / behete them warysoun, 2413
And to bataylle / entre not sodeynly,

<small>be well armed.</small>

but thow haue Armvre / and wepne necessary. 2415

(346)

Vpon thy Enemy / renne not sodeynly, 2416
ne dispurveyed / dreede not for to flee,
What tyme thou art / besegyd traytourly,

[1] In margin of MS.

and the Ordering of War. 77

<blockquote>

ffor dysworshipe / to thy magnanymyte,
It is noon / lerne this of me ; 2420
Keep wel thyn Oost / and the logge al dayes, *Where to lodge your*
Nyhe to hillys / watrys and woodyes.[1] 2422 *army.*

(347)
Haue also greet / Aboundaunce of vitaylle, 2423 [fol. 58 b.]
Moore than the nedith / be lyklynesse ; *Be well victualled,*
ffreshe trompetys / greetly doon avaylle, *and have plenty of trumpets to liven your*
Which to fight / gif greet hardynesse,
Strengthe, vertu / Ioye and lightnesse, 2427 *men.*
Vnto the Oost / which is On thy partye,
And the meny / discounfort / of thy Enemye. 2429

(348)
Be not al tymes / Armyd Oon Armvre, 2430
look thou be kept / wel / with good Archeerys, *Have good archers;*
Summe of thy people / to stand fix and sure,
Othir to Renne vpon / to destroy Arblasteerys, *skirmishers to kill the*
ffair behestys / wyl make fel as steerys, 2434 *arblasteers;*
Wherfore whan thou shalt / entre the bataylle, *remain with the reserves;*
Thy people to Counforte / greetly doth avaylle. 2436

(349)
ffle al hastynesse / in especial chydyng, 2437 *do not find fault;*
And if thorugh tresoun / constreyned thou be to flee,
To haue good hors / swifft of Rennyng, *have a good horse ready to retreat;*
Doth aparteyne / to thyn excellent dignitee,
Which Save thyn Oost / shal and also thee, 2441
ffor thy conservacioun / yf thou resort,
To alle the puissaunce / gevith greet counfort. 2443

(350)
And yif thy Enemyes / gynne for to fle, 2444 [fol. 59 a.]
Chase them not / ovir hastely,
Holde al tyme / togidre thy meyne,
Which shal Cause / the haue victory :
Engynes to haue / is special remedy, 2448 *have siege engines in readiness;*
Yif thou assaylle / wyl Castel or tour,
With maystryes to myne / and special socour. 2450
</blockquote>

[1] 'alway nygh hilles, watirs / & wodys if þu may.'—14408.

Of War, and of Physiognomy.

(351)

poison or destroy their wells;
have skilled spies.

There watrys destroye / or ellys envemyne, 2451
Expert in language / haue explotourys,
Them to be-traye / be sum Sotil Engyne,
And to knowe / alle ther labourys,
A poynt of werre / thoughe vndir flourys, 2455
Of peynted language / reste the scorpioun,
ffor a traytour / to be-traye is no tresoun. 2457

(352)

Lerne this Conclusyoun / folwe my doctrine, 2458
In poyntes of werre / take thyn avayl,

It is better to get what is wanted without war.

And yif thou may / thorugh grace which is dyvyne,
With oute werre / take hede to my Counsayl,
Gete thyn Entent / or withe oute batayl, 2462
Off thyn Enmyes / thou owyst, as sey clerkys,
ffor werre shulde be / the laste of thy werkys.[1] 2464

[fol. 59 b.] **Of the Crafft of physynomye, and the ymage of ypocras.**

(353)

FErthere I wyl / thou knowe in this partye, 2465
the excellent science / celestial and divine,

Philomon, discoverer of physiognomy:

ffounde be philomon / I mene phisonomye,
Be which thou shalt / folwyng my doctryne,
knowe disposicioun / in ech degree and signe, 2469

the use of the science.

Of al thy peple / by polityk prudence,
Which folwe sensuallyte / and which intelligence. 2471

(354)

The qualitees to enserge / and ther naturys, 2472
With othir Crafftys / which that be secree,
Poweer of planetys / in al Creaturys,
Dyfformaciouns / of Circes and medee,
lokyng in facys / lerne this of mee, 2476
And of membrys / to se proporcioun,
Off ech wyght / declaryth the disposicioun. 2478

(355)

In this science / philomon Expert was, 2479
And in al partyes / of philosophie,
In whoos tyme / Regnyd ypocras,

[1] Ar. 59. and Harl. 2251 conclude here.

The Portrait of Hippocrates.

Expert in phesyk / and Astronomye,
Off whoom for purpoos / and ffantasye,
To preve philomon / in his Iugement,
disciples of ypocras / thus did of entent.

(356)
Of moost wyse ypocras / they put in picture,
The ymage / in ech proporcioun,
And to philomon / they Offryd that ffigure,
hym be-sechyng / the disposicioun,
them to telle / with qualitees and condicioun,
Of that man / by his experyence,
Whoos figure they / hadde there in presence.

(357)
Poweer of planetys / and Ek the sterrys,
And of every / hevenly intelligence,
Disposicioun of pees / and Ek of werrys,
And of ech straunge / othir science,
As the sevene goddys / by ther influence,
Or of natural body / the transmutacioun,
Of which he droof / this conclusyoun.

(358)
This man he Seide / of natural resoun,
Was a disceyvour / lovyng leccherye,
ffor which the disciples / in that sesoun,
hym to destroye / purpoosyd ffynally,
And hym rebukyng / with woordys of velony,
They seide " ffool / this ymage prentyd was,
Afftir the ffigure / of moost wyse ypocras."

(359)
This wyse philisoffre / of greet providence,
Wel disposed / seying on this maneer,
With this Resoun / stood at his diffence,
And seide "this ymage / Sovereyn and entieer,
Is of ypocras / ffigure bright and Cleer,
Wherfore I gaff yow / not enformacioun
Of Actual dede / but disposicioun."

(360)
The Answere yove / they passyd his presence,
And to ypocras / yove relacioun,

2483 How Hippocrates' disciples tried Philomon
2485
2486 [fol. 60 a.] with a picture of Hippocrates,
2490
2492
2493 asking his judgment.
2497
2499
2500 He answered that he was deceitful and lecherous.
2504 When they rebuked him angrily,
2506
2507 [fol. 60 b.]
he answered that he told not of deed, but of natural
2511 disposition,
2513
2514

8 *

how they hadde attemptyd / the science
Off wyse philomon / for his disposicioun,

which Hippocrates acknowledged to be true:
Which conceyvyng / his owne Complexioun, 2518
Seide it was trewe / be lyknesse,
Al that of hym / philomon did expresse. 2520

(361)

ffor this dere sone / I wryte in this partye, 2521
Rewlys abreggyd / and sufficient

therefore kings should learn physiognomy.
In the science / of phisonomye,
Which to parceyve / looke thou be dilligent
In alle dowtys / which wyl the Content, 2525
To nature, perteynyng / in substaunce,
And atwen qualitees / make disseveraunce. 2527

(362)

[fol. 61 a.] In sentence breeff / to wryte to thyn honour, 2528
And exclude / al superfluyte,

Avoid washy-looking men. Man which is / feble of Colour
ffor thyn avayl / looke that thou flee,
ffor he is pleynly / tak heed vnto me, 2532
To lecchery dispoosed / be nature and kynde,
And othir evelys / many as I ffynde. 2534

(363)

Choose a man who laughs heartily.
Man which lawheth / with wyl and herte, 2535
Iust / stedfast / and trewe is of nature,

The signs of one who loves you personally.
Oute of thy presence / whych wyll not sterte,
But to be-holde / the deliteth in sure,
Reed, shamefast / witty and demevre, 2539
Which with teerys / and syhyng makith moone,
Whan thou hym blamyst / louyth thy persoone. 2541

(364)

Do not trust deformed persons,
As froom thy Enemy / fle his presence, 2542
Which a-complysshed / in membrys Organychall
Is not / and noote this sentence,
ffor avayl / of thy excellence Royal:
ffroom hym that is / looke thou ffal, 2546

or marked on the face.
Markyd in visage / for lerne this Conclusyoun,
he is disceyvable / by disposicioun. 2548

The Voice; the Ears; the Hair. 81

(365)
Best of Complexioun / to ech Creature,   2549 [fol. 61 b.]
  Is to be / breefly to expresse,
Wel proporciownyd / and meene stature,   *Description of a good appearance;*
  In eyen and heerys / havyng blaknesse,
Colour meene / atwen whyte and Reednesse;   2553
  Visage rounde / boody hool and right,
With meenesse of the heed / is good in ech wyght.   2555

(366)
Meene in voys / nouthir to hih nor baas   2556 *of the voice,*
  In moche speche / which doth noon Offence,
Spekith in tyme / and doth no trespaas
  vnto the Eerys / of the Audience,
Conveieth his mateer / be resoun and prudence,   2560
  In ech Circumstaunce / vsith discrecioun,
Suych a man / is best of complexioun.   2562

(367)
Eerys pleyn and soffte doon signeffye   2563 *of the ears,*
  Man to be boxom / Curteys and kynde,
Coold of brayn / trewthe to speceffye,
  And the Contrarye / conserve this in mynde,
As Eerys sharpe / and thykke, as I ffynde,   2567
  Be evident toknys / and signes palpable,
Of a fool / nyce and varyable.   2569

(368)
Off heer also / whoo hath greete quantite   2570 [fol. 62 a.]
  On wombe and breest / he is, I the sure,   *of the hair,*
Good of condiciouns / in ech signe and gre,
  Merveyllous of complexioun / and singuleer in nature,
In whoos herte / longe doth endure   2574
  Thyng a-geyn Resoun / doo vnfeithfully
To his Rebuke / shame or velony.   2576

(369)
Heerys blake / shewe rightwysnesse   2577 *black hair,*
  In a man / and love and resoun,
The rede also / be signe of ffoolynesse,   *red hair,*
  lak of providence / and discrecioun,
Of fretyng wretthe / with Oute Occasyoun,   2581
PHILOSOPHERS.

G

The Eyes and Eyebrows.

And Colour a-twen both / to speke breefly
Of pesable man / is signe and witty.   2583

(370)

large eyes, And he that hath / Eeyen Out of mesure   2584
Ovir greete / with oute proporcio*u*n,
He is in voys / of kynde and nature,
Slaw, vnshamefast / with oute subieccio*u*n;
A-twen bothe / which kepe dymencio*u*n,   2588
colour of eyes, Of Colour browñ / nouthir blak nor whyte,
Curteys trewe / and konnyng be of right.   2590

(371)

[fol. 62 b.] Eeyen longe / and extendid visage,   2591
long eyes, Signe be / of malice and Envye;
Dul of cheer / which lyst nat to rage,
But as the Asse / evir casteth his Eeye
To the Erthe / tak heed of this partye: 2595
He is a fool / malicious, vntretable,
Hard of kynde / and not sociable.   2597

(372)

shifty eyes. Eeyen also / which be lightly mevyng,   2598
visage long / with oute mesure,
Off hasty man / vntrewe and levyng,
Be signes Evident / and tooknys I the sure;
Colour reed / Causyd of blood pure,   2602
Is signe of strengthe / and greet manlynesse,
Which to fight / gevith greet hardynesse.   2604

(373)

But of this mateere / looke thou heede take,   2605
Spots round the eyes the very worst sign. That werst signe / in disposicio*u*n
Is whan spottys / reede, whyte, or blake,
Mannys Eeyes / doo enviro*u*n,
Werst of othir / with oute comparyso*u*n;   2609
Thick eye-brows. And whoo so heer / thykke doth bere
On the browys / is a shrewd spekere.   2611

(374)

[fol. 63 a.] fferthere, whoo hath / moche heer dependyng   2612
the eyebrows, A-twene the browes / is a shrewd signe,
Browys large / to templys / ech strecchyng,

Signe of hym / that falsnesse wyl mayntyne ;
Which keepe meene / tak heed of my doctryne, 2616
And in mooche heer / be not Aboundyng,
Evident signe be / of good vndirstandyng. 2618

(375)
Noote this mateer / Entitle it Redily, 2619
long noose / strecchyng vnto the mouth, *long noses,*
Tokne is of man / boold and hardy,
And he that hath / the nature that is vnkouth,
Cammyd nose / bore in north or south, 2623 *camuse nose,*
With gristil of nose / litel redily,
Is sone wroth / hoot and hasty. 2625

(376)[1]
fferthere take heed / to my doctryne, 2626
large nose in myddys / which doth vp ryse, *large hooked nose.*
Of a lyere / and greet spekyng is signe,
As Oold philisoffres / Clerly doth devise;
But best he is / in ech maner wyse. 2630
That nose-thrylles / ne[2] nose, I the hete,
Ovir litel hath / ne Ovir greete. 2632

(377)
In this mateere / ferthere to procede, 2633 [fol. 63 b.]
And it Entitle / vnto thy good grace,
Moo of membrys / to the it is nede
Propirtees to knowe / in special of the fface,
Dirk ignoraunce / awey which wyl chace ; 2637
Which plat and pleyn / though it be specious, *An envious face.*
Is signe Evident / of man Envious. 2639

(378)
Signes be / for ful conclusyoun, 2640
As in wryting / philisoffres seyn,
Whan face kepith / dew proporcioun,
These dymenciouns / he kepith in certeyn,
Not engrosyd / nouthir ovir pleyn, 2644 *A well-proportioned face.*
Jawys and templys / in mene vp-rysyng,
Which signe is / of witt / and greet vndirstandyng. 2646

[1] Not in Lansd. 285.   [2] 'the' in MS.

(379)

The voice,	Meene in voys / neythir to grete nor smalle,	2647
	Signe is of trewthe / and rightwysnesse,	
	Whoo spekith soone / or ony man hym calle	
	Is vnresounable / as philisoffres expresse:	
	Greet voys / signe of hastynesse,	2651
	Greet sownyng / Envyous and Angry,	
	ffair and hih / of wyldenesse and ffooly.	2653

(380)

[fol. 64 a.]	Considre / Alysaundre / be dilligent labour,	2654
moving of hands,	Whoo in talkyng / Conceyve what I mene,	
	Handys doth meve / is a disceyvour,	
	He stant stable / from these is pure and clene;	
small neck,	With nekke to smal / in proporcioun whoo be sene	2658
	Is a fool / ovir short / disceyvable,	
	And ovir gross / A lyeer detestable.	2660

(381)

"good round belly,"	And he that hath / wombe greet withoute mesure,	2661
	Proud, lecherous, is / and vnprudent,	
	breest greet, and shuldrys / large insure,	
well shaped body,	With bak wel shape / be signes Evident	
	Of many wourthy / wys and provident,	2665
	Good of vndirstandyng / hardy to fight,	
	Who hath the Contrary / is noyous to ech wyght.	2667

(382)

long arms,	Armys longe / strecchyng to the knee,	2668
	Tokne of wysdam / is and hardynesse;	
sharp shoulders,	Shuldrys sharpe / I mene not reysed with slevys,	
	Off evyl feith / is lyklynesse,	
long fingers,	longe fyngerys / trewthe to expresse,	2672
	Crafftys to lerne / yevith disposicioun,	
	In Especial / of manual Operacioun.	2674

(383)

[fol. 64 b.]	He that hath ffyngres / greet and shoort	2675
thick. short fingers,	Is dispoosed / noote this doctryne,	
	To be a fool / nyce in his dispoort;	
great feet,	Whoo hath greet feet / vntrewthe wyl mayntyne,	
small feet	litel and light / been evident sigue	2679

The twelve Signs of a good Man.

That he is hard / of vndirstandyng,
And smale leggys / be tokne of symple konnyng. 2681 *and legs,*

(384)
Of leggys and helys / be tokenyth largenesse 2682
Mighty to be / in strength of body;
In knees also / trewthe to expresse, *knees.*
He that is ovir / moche fflesshy,
Is soffte and feble / lerne this naturally; 2686
Whoo hath litel / is evil of wyl,
In al thynges / hasty with oute skyl. 2688

(385)
To al vertu / disposed, and science, 2689
Good and kynde / of Complexioun,
Is a man / havyng in sentence
Signes twelve / be computacioun; *Twelve signs*
fflesshe soffte / of disposicioun, 2693 *of a good man.*
Or meenely sharp / and of mene stature.
Twen whyte and Reed / in Colour kepith mesure. 2695

(386)
Swete of look / and the Eerys pleyn, 2696 [fol. 65 *a*.]
Eyen menely / grete be mesure,
The heed not greet / but a-twen tweyn,
Moche and litel / is good I the sure;
Nekke sufficient / and of good stature, 2700
Whos shuldrys bowe / a litel mesurably,
In leggis nor kneeys / be not moche fflesshy. 2702

(387)
Cleer of voys / and eke mesurable, 2703
Palmys and ffyngrys / longe in suffysaunce,
Skornys to vse / is not comendable,
lawhyng visage / is good in daliaunce,
vsyd in mene / With dew Circumstaunce; 2707
ffor afftir the mateer / requerith audience,
So contenaunce to shewe / is good providence. 2709

(388)
Be oon in-sight / deme no man to soone, 2710 *Note all the members,*
In sentence breeff / folwe my doctryne,
ffor hasty demyng / where men haue to doone,

86 — *Do not judge by one Feature.*

<small>and do not draw conclusions from one alone.</small>

  Of improvidence / is evident signe ;
  And this book / breffly to termyne,   2714
  In oon membir / for ful conclusyoun,
  nevir deme / mannys disposicioun.   2716

(389)

[fol. 65 b.] Behoold al¹ signes / give aduertence,   2717
  Which moost aboundyn / to se is avaylable,
  And in mynde / by polityk prudence,
  nombre of them / which be most profitable,
  In party best / and moost Amyable,   2721
  Which the mvt graunte / the lord moost imperial

<small>Explicit.³</small> Aboue al hevenys / Supra celestial. Amen.   2723

(390)

<small>Lenvoye.²</small> Goo litel book / and mekely me excuse,   2724
  To alle thoo that / shal the seen or rede,
  Yf ony man / thy Rudnesse lyst accuse,
  Make no diffence / but with lowlyhede
  Pray hym refourme / wheer as he seth nede :   2728
  To that entent / I do the forth directe,
  Wher thou fayllest / that men shal the correcte.   2730

  ¹ 'of' MS.   ² Not in this MS

NOTES.

p. 1, l. 1. This Introduction is taken advantage of by some to insert the name of the king by whose orders the translation is made. Thus Shirley dedicates his translation to Henry VI, and the French translation in the king's library, printed in 1489, is dedicated to Charles VIII. The first twenty lines are Lydgate's summary of the duties of a king, founded on a couple of lines in the original, "Deus omnipotens custodiat regem nostrum ad gloriam credentium, et confirmet regnum suum ad tuendam legem divinam suam, et perdurare faciat ipsum ad exaltandum honorem et laudem bonorum."

ll. 1—300 represent the prologue in the Arabic version, with the exception of 211—231, which are due to a mistake in some Latin MSS., which substitute the name of Philip of Paris for Jahja ibn al Batrik.

p. 1, l. 8. The lord = God.

p. 1, l. 20. 'In your desire this processe for to here.'—*Ass. of Lad.* 27.
'I make an ende of this prosses.'—*B. D. s. M.* 848.
'And shortly of this processe for to pace.'—*Leg. Ariadne* 29.
'What wise I should perform the said processe
Considiryng by gode avisement
My unconnyng and my grete simplenesse
And ayenward the straite commaundement.'—*B. D. s. M.* 158.
'Of this processe now forth will I procede.'
Balade In Feverere 22.
'Takith at gre,' 'To take at gre.'—*T. of Glas* 1085.

p. 1, l. 21. 'By ther favour and supportacioun
To take in gre this rude Translacioun.'—*B. D. s. M.* 840.
'Accept in gre this litil short tretesse.'—*C. of L.* 28.

rudness of my style.
'Thy rude langage full boystously unfold.'—*F. and L.* 595.

p. 1, l. 24. 'Voyde of Elloquence.'
'With timerous herte & trembling hand of drede
Of cunning nakid, bare of eloquence.'—*C. of L.* 1.
'Destitute
Of Eloquence.'—*B. D. s. M.* 842.

p. 2, l. 33. *digne* refers to *book* in 31.

p. 2, l. 46. The Arabic and most Latin versions have 'bicornis' or 'duo cornua habuisse dicitur.' The two horns are due to the two horns with which his God-father Ammon is represented. See *Wars of Alexander*, p. 10. Ed. E. E. T. S.

p. 3, l. 77. Lydgate's text only justified him in saying that some of the philosophers had counted Aristotle a prophet.

p. 4, l. 89. *Vnkouth and strange*, 'extranea opera.' See l. 219.
'Uncouth and straung.'—*Ch. Dream.* 1427.

p. 4, l. 98. *dowe.* Lat. 'columna,' which in some MSS. is columbn. Fr. columbe. Shirley, culvour. This opinion is attributed to the peripatetics.

p. 4, l. 104. *Al hool the world,* a common use. See l. 196, &c.
'All whole in govirnance.'—*C. of L.* 373.
'Had whole achievid th' obeysaunce.'—*Ch. Dr.* 2.
'Whole your thought.'—*Ch. Dr.* 498.

p. 4, l. 110. *The Round bal.* When was the orb introduced as a royal sign?

Septemtryoun. Several MSS. speak of Alexander, 'qui dominatus fuit toti orbi, dictusque monarcha in Septentrione.' I don't see why 'in septentrione.'

p. 4, l. 112. *vij Clymatys.* The world was divided into seven climates by ancient geographers, such as Ptolemy. These were divisions answering to the length of the longest day. Thus the first climate was from the Equator to where the longest day was 12 hrs. 45 mins., and was named the Climate of Meröes. The second was called from Syenes, the longest day was 13¼ hrs.; the third from Alexandria, 13¾ hrs.; the fourth Rhodes, 14¼ hrs.; the fifth Rome, 14¾ hrs.; the sixth from the Black Sea, 15¼ hrs.; and the seventh, North Germany, 15¾ hrs., the rest of the world being reputed uninhabitable. The climates south of the Equator were called anti-Meröen, &c. &c. However, more modern writers divide the space between the Equator and the Arctic Circle in twenty-four climates, allowing a half-hour difference of longest day to each climate. See *Cluverij. Introductione in Universam Geographiam,* Lib. VII.; *Amst. Elz.* 1659. 12°. p. 22; *Borrhaus in Cosmographiae Elementa. Bas.* 1555. 8°. p. 121, &c. &c.

p. 5, l. 113. *grucchyng.* 'Grutching in no wyse.'—*C. of L.* 960.
'Withoutin grutchinge or rebellion.'—*Pilgrim.* 183 b; *Troy-Book,* Bb, d; *Comp. of Bk. Kt.* 554; *L. Lady* f, a; *T. of Glas* 424, 879.

p. 5, l. 147. *the ffyn of ther entent.*
'The fine of his entente.'—*T. and C.* iii. 125.

p. 5, l. 150. *magnanymyte.* This expresses a quality not readily expressible in English. Cf. Freeman's *History of William Rufus.* These were men 'quorum actiones in regiam potentiam directae sunt.'

p. 6, l. 155. Lydgate alters his text, which expresses a desire to slay them.

p. 6, l. 160. The text might equally well be Jupartye, but it seems to me that the sense of *imparting* information would do better. The other texts are little guide to what Lydgate would write. The English is, 'But only thou certifie vs bi thi lettres, as thou seemest most spedfulle vnto vs'; the Latin is, 'Quidquid igitur super hoc decreveris, nobis significa tuis scriptis'; the Arabic is, 'What do you advise in this matter?'

p. 6, l. 164. Lydgate here entirely misapprehends the sense of his text, which is that if Alexander can change the air and water of that land, and the disposition of their states, then he was to fulfil his intention; meaning, 'since you can't change the nature of the country, govern it by kindness.'

p. 6, l. 166. An allusion to the spheres of the elements. See quotation in note on line 551. They were supposed to lie immediately round the earth, which was the sphere of earth, then came air, then water, and outside that fire. Then followed the planetary spheres. But *Bart. Angl. de Prop. Rerum* puts it otherwise; see my *Medieval Lore* for some account of medieval astronomy according to him.

p. 7, l. 186. *wynges.* A favourite Middle Age symbol for the protection of a king, &c., derived from Scriptural sources. See l. 324, 'wynges of humble Obedyence.'

p. 7, l. 204. Freinsheim, in his supplement to *Quintus Curtius*, Lib. I., cap. iii., had this in mind when he wrote 'Eam autem Philosophiae partem, quae sibi aliis que probe imperare docet, ita coluit, ut magnanimitate, prudentia, temperantia, fortitudine, quam armis et opibus instructior, tantam imperii Persici molem subruere agressus censeatur.'

p. 7, l. 210. The mistake of attributing this to Philip of Paris arises from a shortened Latin copy, which put Philip of Tripoli's heading, and omitted his dedicatory letter to Bishop Guido. Paris seems to have been arrived at from reading the contracted form of 'Patricii' as 'Parisii.' There is no Philip of Paris who can be found likely to have had anything to do with this work.

p. 7, l. 220. *sugryd enspyred Elloquence.* See l. 376.
'A word of sugrid eloquence.'—*C. of L.* 933.
'Of Tullius had the sugrid eloquence.'
     Lydgate's balade of good conseil 100.
'sugred dytees.'—*Troy-Book* G_s a.
'sugred eloquence.'—*Troy-Book* K_s d.
'The sugred language.'—*Falls of Pr.* 163 d.

p. 8, l. 224. *Tullius gardyn.*
'The blosomes fresh of Tulius gardein sote.'—*C. of L.* 8.

p. 8, l. 227. *wakir goos. Parl. Foules,* st. 52.

p. 8, l. 232. Lines 232 to 301 are repeated, 603—37 more compactly. The Arabic very curiously represents Jahja ibn al Batrik as searching all the temples of the *Egyptians.* The differences between the two versions show us Lydgate getting over the ground, or pausing to amplify every thought, and the results.

p. 8, l. 246. *Cupydes ffyr,* learning under the guise of love.

p. 8, l. 249. *Cytheroes tonne.* Is this a reference to the vats of sweet and bitter, of which each of us may take one ? 'licour.'
'O auriate licour of Clio! to write.'—*Balade in comendacioun,* &c., 13.

p. 9, ll. 250-5, 59, 282, &c. Here the mention of the temple of the sun leads him to use the sun as a metaphor for knowledge.
'ʒoure stremes clere.'—*T. of Glas* 1342.
'And Phebus with his bemis clere.'—*In praise of women,* l. 26.

p. 10, l. 301. *Chalde.* Syriac. The Arabic calls it 'recent' (Roman), but gives no hint as to the leader of the faithful the translation was made for.

p. 10, l. 302. This stanza is Lydgate speaking for himself, and introducing the prolog of Philip of Tripoli.

p. 10, l. 309. ll. 310-11 depend on *hym,* 312 *et seq.* follow *drough.*

p. 10, l. 314. *Celestial,* a rather badly chosen epithet.

p. 11, l. 317. *Covalence.* Lydgate makes Valence into Covalence, for the sake of the verse.

p. 11, l. 318. Metropolitan is a misreading of Tripolitanus. Some poor MSS. have 'tropol,' which Lydgate might have conjectured into Metropolitanae.

p. 11, l. 319, is substantially repeated in 327.

p. 11, l. 321. The seven sciences are Mathematics, Geometry, Astronomy, Music, Ethics, Physics and Metaphysics. The seven arts are Grammar, Dialectics and Rhetoric (the trivium), and Arithmetic, Music, Geometry and Astronomy (the quadrivium), but the distinction was lost in Lydgate's time. The seven arts are characters in the *Court of Sapience.* See l. 1527. There were also seven prohibited arts, and seven mechanic arts—Lanificium, Armatura, Navigatio, Agricultura, Venatio, Medicina, and Theatrica.

p. 11, l. 322. *Phillipus*, not of Paris, but of Tripoli.
p. 11, l. 331. *Astonyd.* Astond—not Astonied—fixed, firm.
p. 11, l. 334. *With quakyng penne*, &c., a favourite Lydgate phrase.
'Quakith my penne—my spirit supposeth,
That in my writing ye find woll offence.'
Mother of norture, 50-1, and see *T. of Glas.*
p. 11, l. 337. *I have no Colour but oonly Chalk & sable.*
'or colouris of rhetorike.'—*H. of F.* ii. 351.
p. 11, ll. 341-8. *lych as the moone passith a smal sterre.*
'As of light the somer sonne shene
Passeth the sterre.'—*Parl. of F.* 299.
'As the somer sonne
Passeth the sterre with his bemes shene.'
Flour of C. 113; *T. of Glas* 251, 252.
p. 11, l. 343. *Arthurus and the sterrys sevene.* The Pole star Arcturus and the Great Bear. This is higher in the scheme of spheres than the seven planets.
p. 11, l. 347. *fervent as the glede.*
'A thousande sighis hottir than the glede.'—*T. and C.* iv. 337.
p. 12, l. 352. *Ceryously*, unusual for 'in series.'
p. 12, l. 372. The next seventy lines Lydgate builds on the following—
'Adhuc in in scientris liberalibus literalissimus, in Ecclesiasticis et legibus peritissimus, in divinis et moralibus doctissimus.' One shudders to think what might have been if he had gone through the whole work in this way.
p. 12, l. 378. Like Chrysostom.
p. 13, l. 384. Perhaps Lydgate had in mind the famous Aurora, a medieval compendium of divinity by Peter of Riga, a canon of Rheims (1209), and combined this reminiscence with the meaning of daybreak.
p. 13, l. 397. The same metaphor of Phebus for clearness, &c., as in ll. 250, &c.
p. 14, l. 414. *the hevenly influence* was the favourable aspect of the stars.
'The seven planets discending fro the spheres
Whiche hath powir of al thing generable
To rule and stere by ther gret influence
Wedir & wind, and course variable.'—*Test. of Cres.* 147.
p. 14, l. 424. Seven Wells of Philosophy. Who first used this figure?
p. 14, l. 430. See l. 722.
p. 14, l. 431. Lucan was one of the most popular poets in medieval times, due perhaps to his supernatural machinery and to the subject. He is one of the pillars in the *House of Fame*, iii. 407—16.
p. 14, l. 442. Antioch in *Greece*.
p. 14, l. 444. The Latin speaks of 'this most precious pearl of philosophy.' Lydgate likes a ruby better.
'Geme of beaute! O carbuncle shining pure!'—*Craft of Lovers* 33.
'No rube riche of price.'—*C. of Love* 78.
'A fyn charboncle sette saugh I,
The stone so clere was and so bright,
That, also soone as it was nyght,
Men myghte seen to go for nede
A myle or two, in lengthe and brede.'—*Rom. of Rose.*
Neckham and Bartholomew also speak of its shining at night. See l. 552.
p. 14, l. 447. The assonance 'sent of assent.'

Notes to Pages 15, 16; Lines 454—495.

p. 15, l. 454. *humble Affeccyoun.* There is nothing of the modern sense of affection here. It is humble disposition, 'cupiens humiliter obedire.'

p. 15, l. 459. A Lydgate sentiment, taken from wood-cutting,—a dangerous and unhandy way of working, 'Yet since there were but few copies even among the Arabs themselves, he would try to translate it.'

p. 15, l. 469. *magnanymyte*, mistake for 'magnitudinem,' your greatness.

p. 15, l. 476. This rubric is put in without any reason; the next few stanzas are a continuation of Philip of Tripoli's prologue.

p. 16, ll. 477—483. These lines are manifestly worthless. They have neither beginning nor end, and do not join to the next. Evidently put here by Burgh because there was no other place but l. 638 perhaps.

p. 16, l. 485. *a purpose take*, &c., 'took a purpose.' l. 486 is in a parenthesis. The Latin is, 'Qui postulavit ab eo, ut ad ipsum veniret et secreta quarundam artium sibi fideliter revelaret, videlicet motum, operationem et potestatem astrorum in astronomia, et artem alchemiae in natura, et artem cognoscendi naturas, et operandi incantationes et celimantiam et geomantiam.'

p. 16, l. 491. See p. 79, ll. 2493—2498, where the lines are used again.

p. 16, ll. 491-3, are references to the astrological part of Alexander's secrets.

p. 16, l. 495. The seven gods are the seven planets. It is a part of Lydgate's learning to put them under this form.

The process of incantations in Lydgate's time was long and interesting. Suppose, for example, you want to bring anybody to a violent death, you will then want to call up the Evil Spirit of Mars. Get yourself up as a priest, or at least in clean linen vestments; prepare a pentacle, and trace it out with a consecrated sword; mark in the corners a number of sacred emblems, and then commence by asking God's blessing on the work. Then get a friend with you to read the proper lesson, and call up all the good spirits of the day to be near you. Then conjure Mars to appear under any form he thinks fit. If he is coming you will see a burning flame approach you, thunder and lightning will surround the circle, he will roar like mad bulls, and have stag's horns and griffin's claws. At last he will appear, either as an armed king riding on a wolf, or a woman holding a shield on her thigh, or a goat, or a horse, or a stag, or a red cloak, or as wool, or some one of a number of other shapes. Then command him to do what you will, and then order him to go quietly. Perhaps he won't, and then you have to pile on the imprecations till he is frightened. Very likely, however, he may not become visible at all, but don't think he is not there. If you leave your pentacle unwarily, you will most likely be torn to pieces. The safest thing to do is to keep on conjuring him till he comes, and then to send him away. Then you have to call all the good spirits you can to your aid, and when you feel you have sufficient near you, to leave the place and get home. Of course you have to choose a favourable spot. Near an old execution ground, or battlefield, is the best one for Mars. Some authors recommend making another pentacle beside your own, and conjuring the spirit into that, but then there is quite literally the devil to pay when you let him out.

'Sith that I se the brighte goddis seven.'—*Visage without paintyng.* See *Test. of Cres.* 147 (note on l. 414).

'Gan thankin tho the blissful goddis seven.'—*T. and C.*, iii. 1203.

'And clerkis eke which connin well
All this magike hight Naturell,
That craftily doe ther ententes
To maken in certain ascendentes,' &c.—*H. of Fame*, iii. 175.

p. 16, l. 497. The seven metals date from the earliest times. They are electrum (a natural alloy of gold and silver, counting as one of them), gold, silver, copper, iron, tin, and lead. Proclus, in his commentary on the Timaeus, refers some metals to the planets: gold to the sun, silver to the moon, lead to Saturn, and iron to Mars. Olympiodorus (see *Fab. Bibl. Graec.*, V. vi.) gives the complete list: electrum to Jupiter, copper to Venus, tin to Hermes, and the others as above. When it was perfectly clear that electrum was not a metal, but an alloy, tin was assigned to Jupiter, and quicksilver was appropriated to Mercury. There does not seem to have been much distinction made between brass and copper in early times—probably they had no pure copper, but such as was found native.

p. 16, l. 498. This line repeated, l. 2473.

p. 16, l. 499. Calculations and Geomancye. Calculations were such things as our wheel of fortune, fortune-telling cards, &c. Geomancy was originally the scattering of grains of sand on the ground, and afterwards came to the scattering of blots on a sheet of paper from a pen. There were sixteen shapes to which these blots were approximated, such as Journey, Prison, Girl, Boy, Head, Fortune, &c. &c.—*H. C. Agrippa de Oc. Phil.*, II. xlviii.

The most modern form of geomancy is tea-cup tossing, an art not lost in our womankind of the middle class.

p. 16, l. 500. See l. 2475. A Chaucer line, *K. T.* 1086.

p. 16, l. 501. Looking on faces, Physiognomy. See the story of Democritus and the maid.

Piromancye is Pyromancy, the art of prediction from fire, not only from comets, &c., but also glows in coals, and rushes of fire. There were four leading sorts of divination, 'Varro dicit divinationis quatuor esse genera, terram, aquam, aerem, signem.'—*Isidore Orig.*, VIII. 9.

Geomancy included originally the art of divination from earth tremblings, as hydromantia and aeromantia were presages from water and air respectively. These are added by Lydgate to Philip's list.

p. 17, l. 512. One does not exactly see the bearing of 'writing woord.' Otherwise the remark is a commonplace of the doctrine of signatures, beginning then to be of great importance.

p. 17, l. 516. Cast. Cf. 'Cast about.'

p. 17, l. 518. *sette his herte at Ese.*

'yet sette mine herte in rest.'—*C. of L.* 1022.

'that maie her herte appese.'—*C. of L.* 397.

'In this mattir to set your herte in pese.'—*B. D. s. M.* 252.

p. 17, ll. 519—588, seem to have been composed as a sort of general summary of Lydgate's, probably sent to some person with a view to awakening curiosity as to the scope of the book. At any rate they do not come in here, and are founded partly, as ll. 988—1008 are, on cap. 67 of the Latin version.

p. 17, l. 527. The mysteries Lydgate here speaks of are such as are preserved for us by Albertus Magnus in the translations made for him from the Arabic in his *Liber Aggregationis*, of the virtues of herbs, stones, and animals. He treats first of the occult virtues of sixteen plants, and further of seven more attributed to the seven planets by Alexander the emperor, but not included in the *Secreta Secretorum*. The second book treats of the virtues of stones, of which he names forty-six, and his third treats of eighteen animals. There are very few stories of the use of fish in magic. Tobit's fish is almost unique.

p. 17, l. 530. These stones were at first compounds used in medicine; then in the time of the *Secreta*, or soon after, became theoretical expositions of alchemy, and then seemed to have been refined away. I have no doubt but that originally compounds were made from these three sources, animal, vegetable, and mineral, *e. g.* bezoar, coral, &c.; and, even in the 17th century, we find continually that people were compounding mixtures out of dung, with the idea of getting the elixir out of it. Later on, stone in alchemy did not mean stone, but compound.

p. 17, l. 530. 'Tres sunt lapides, et tres sales sunt, ex quibus totum magisterium consistit: Scilicet mineralis, plantalis, & animalis. Et sunt tres aquae, scilicet Solaris, Lunaris, & Mercurialis. Mercurius est minera, Luna planta, quia recipit in se duos colores, albedinem et rubedinem. Et Sol est animalis, quia recepit tria, scilicet constrictionem, albedinem, & rubedinem, & vocatur animal magnum.'—*Rosarium Philosophorum*, p. 259.

The *Secreta Secretorum* only speaks of two stones.

p. 17, l. 535. The word 'Element' does not bear the signification which we now attach to it, of being a presumably primary form of matter, but refers to the ancient division of bodies according to their primary qualities, hot, cold, moist and dry. These qualities could exist two by two in the simplest form of bodies imaginable, as cold and moist, which was then named Water, not as being anything resembling actual water, but because that representing these qualities was a convenient class name.

'Lapis dicitur habere quatuor elementa, quae exponit Arnolfus. Quia cum facta est solutio, dicitur unum elementum, scilicet aqua. Et cum corpus est immundum, dicitur secundum elementum, scilicet terra. Et cum est calcinata dicta terra, dicitur ignis: et cum iterum solutus est lapis, dicitur aer.'—*Rosarium Philosophorum*. (A cento from Arab chemists, not later than 13th century translation) in *Artis Auriferae*, II., p. 288, Bas. 1572, 8°.

p. 17, l. 536. See notes on ll. 988, *et seq.* Here Lydgate may not mean 'in equal proportions,' but 'in just proportion.'

p. 17, l. 539. 'that men reden in the lapidaire.'—*H. of Fame*, iii. 262. Many medieval collections circulated under this name. See Marbodius 'de Gemmis,' Evax, Albertus Magnus quoted above, Trithemius, Cardan, Bartholomew Anglicus, Pliny, and many others.

p. 17, l. 541. The relation of Lydgate to the alchemical revival in the reign of Henry VI. The editor has published in *The Antiquary*, Sept. 1891, a number of legal documents and commissions illustrating this revival, from which it is evident that from 1444 to 1480 there was great activity in the study of alchemy. That Lydgate himself, if the ballad is his, knew some alchemists is evident from the following extract from Harl. 2251, 20 v°.

'The Alkamystre / tretith of mynaralles
And of metalles / transmutaciouns,
Of sulphur, mercury / Aloms and of sallis,
And of theyre sundry / generaciouns:
What is cause / of theyr coniunxtions,
Why some be clene / some leperous and nat able,
ffixing of spirites / with sublymacions:
Thus euery thyng / drawith to his semblable.'

That popular tradition associated alchemy with his name is evident from the prose treatise in Sl. 3708 being attributed to him.

The works of the celebrated alchemist, Raymund Lully, were translated into Latin, from Catalan, in London at the Priory of St. Bartholomew by Lambert G——; and the Editor's copy in MS. gives the date 6th June, 1443. Later on, alchemy grew to such a point that Henry VI. appointed three Royal

Note to Page 17; *Line* 541.

Commissions to inquire into the subject, from one of which an extract is given, showing the aim of the alchemy of the time:

1456. 34 H. VI., m. 7.

'The king, etc., Greeting.

Know ye that in former times wise and famous Philosophers in their writings and books, under figures and coverings, have left on record and taught, that from wine, from precious stones, from oils, from vegetables, from animals, from metals, and the cores of minerals, many glorious and notable medicines can be made; and chiefly, that most precious medicine which some Philosophers have called the Mother and Empress of Medicines; others have named it the priceless glory, others have called it the Quintessence, others the Philosophers' Stone and Elixir of Life; of which potion the efficacy is so certain and wonderful, that by it all infirmities whatsoever are easily curable, human life is prolonged to its natural limit, and man wonderfully preserved in health and manly strength both of body and mind, in vigour of limbs, clearness of memory, and perspicacity of talent to the same period; All kinds of wounds, too, which may be cured, are healed without difficulty, and in addition it is the best and surest remedy against all kinds of poisons; with it, too, many other advantages most useful to us and to the Commonwealth of our kingdom can be wrought, as the transmutation of metals into actual Gold and the finest Silver.'

Archbishop Neville, who died in 1470, was a great supporter of the alchemists; and one of his clients, Sir George Ripley, has left a picture of the false alchemists of the time. It seems that the sanctuary at Westminster was one of their haunting places. Ripley describes how they are hunted about the city of London:

'Folys doe folow them at the tayle,
Promotyd to ryches wenyng to be;'

Merchants and goldsmiths lay watch for them,

'Wenyng to wyn so grete tresure
That ever in ryches they shall endure.'

But some lenders would be glad to see their goods again, and arrest the alchemists by the 'Sarjaunts':

'But when the Sarjaunts do them arest,
Ther Paukeners be stuffed wyth Parrys balls;
Or wyth Sygnetts of Seynt Martynes at the lest,
But as for Mony yt ys pyssyd on the walls:
Then be they led as well for them befalls
To Newgate or Ludgate as I yon tell,
Because they shall in safeguard dwell.'

Then they are questioned:

'"Where ys my Mony becom?" seyth one,
"And where ys myne?" seyth he and he.'

And the result is, they talk over their creditors:

'Dotyng the Merchaunts, that they be fayne
To let them go, but ever in vayne:'

And off they go to Westminster, where the Archdeacon is so good to them:

'And when they there syt at the wyne,
These Monkys (they sey) have many a pound,
Wolde God (seyth one) that som were myne;
"Hay hoe, care away, lat the cup go rounde:"
"Drynk on," seyth another, "the mene ys founde:
I am a Master of that Arte,
I warrant us we shall have parte."'

Note to Page 17; Line 541.

And so they do, for the monks believe in them; 'some bring a mazer, and some a spoon'; and Ripley ironically advises the Abbot to support people who know so well how to bring back his monks to the pristine poverty of St. Benedict.

There is some possibility that Burgh himself may have been a student of alchemy in his later years. There is a poem in the *Theatrum Chemicum Britannicum* of Ashmole, attributed to the Vicar of Malden, which may have been written in the reign of Edward IV. by Burgh, who would be recognized by his best-known work, the *Distichia Moralia*, as Vicar of Maldon. Ashmole himself refers the work to an otherwise unknown Andrews.

The *Secreta Secretorum* is alluded to—without showing any knowledge of it—in the Canon's Yeoman's Tale as 'Secree of secrees' (16915). In Chaucer's time no other secrets were thought of but the secrets of alchemy. It would seem that the alchemy of the *Secreta* dates back to an early period, and that it becomes prominent in the English version only because of the suppression of the remainder of the section in which it occurs, which deals with the supernatural properties of gems, and of incantations. It is, quite obviously, purely theoretical; and if it is compared with the work of Djaber Al Koufi (Geber), who wrote on alchemy at about the same time, the distinction is most clearly marked. The Aristotelian division of elements, on which the chapter in this work is founded, is purely a theoretical conception, and no one thought of isolating them in old times, more than a modern expects to isolate the ether of our physical speculations. Yet the crude notion of separating, purifying, and combining these elements is just what a man who wished to introduce the subject into a chapter on marvels would form and put down. On the other hand, if the alchemical notions are cruder, the expectations indulged were less high-flown. Gower, in the 4th book of his *Confessio Amantis* (ii. 86-7, ed. Pauli, 1857), speaks of the three stones thus, and he will explain our author best, as he is but amplifying his words.

'These olde Philosophres wyse,
By wey of kinde in sondry wise;
Thre Stones made through Clergy,
The firste, if I shall specify,
Was cleped *Vegetabilis;*
Of which the propre vertue is,
To mannes hele for to serve,
As for to keepe, and to preserve
The body fro sikenesses alle,
Till deth of kinde upon hym falle.
'The seconde Stone I the behote
Is *Lapis Animalis* hote:
The whose vertue, is propre and couth,
For Ere and Eye, and Nase and Mouth;
Whereof a man may here, and se,
And smelle and taste, in his degre.
And for to fele and for to go,
It helpeth a man, of bothe two:
The wittes five he underfongeth[1]
To keepe, as it to hym belongeth.
'The thridde Stone in speciall
by name is cleped *Minerall*,
Which the Metalles of every mine,
Attempreth, till that thei ben fine;

[1] Undertakes, takes in hand.

     'And pureth hem by such a wey,
     That all the vice goth awey,
     Of Rust, of Stynke, and of Hardnesse:
     And when they ben of such clennesse,
     This minerall, so as I finde,
     Transformeth all the firste kinde,
     And maketh hem able to conceive,
     Through his vertue, and receive
     Both in substaunce and in figure,
     Of Gold and Silver the nature.'

 p. 17, l. 544. Much of the practical alchemy of this time was devoted to the fabrication of precious stones.

 p. 18, l. 545. A literal quotation from the Latin text.

 p. 18, l. 548. *medle of.* Note the Latinism. Some writers have doubted Lydgate's knowledge of Latin.
 = 'at *my* presumption.'

 p. 18, l. 551. *above the nyne sperys.* 'Et novem sunt coeli unum infra aliud, infra se invicem: prior ergo et superior spherarum est sphera circundans Deum ipsum sphera siderum. Secunda postque jam sphera est Saturni: et sic usque ad spheram lunae: infra quam est sphera ellementorum quattuor: quae sunt ignis, aer, aqua, et terra.'—*Sec. Sec.*, c. 76. But no two writers arrange the nine spheres alike.

 p. 18, l. 552. 'Carbunculus is a precious stone, and shyneth as fyre / whose shynynge is not overcomme by night. It shyneth in derke places / and it semeth as hit were a flame.'—*Barth. Angl.*, xvi. 26. Trevisa's transl., ed. 1535, f. 228 *a*. It seems to be a popular error that the ruby shines by night, though by means of a properly constructed machine, a true phosphorescence of the ruby has been observed. Lydgate's idea of transferring the ruby to a shrine is, I think, good. See l. 444.

 p. 18, l. 555. 'putte my sylff in prees,' to enter into contest. Cf. French *aux prises.*
    'How darst thou put thyself in prees for drede?'—*F. and L.* 592.

 p. 18, l. 556. A favourite metaphor drawn from initiation ceremonies in all time.

 p. 18, l. 561 *et seq.* This stanza proves how much the doctrine of the four elements had been departed from in Lydgate's time. It is as who should say now, 'Separate from tin its atomic weight, atomic heat, conductivity, and other physical and chemical properties (naming them one by one); make each of these qualities equal to the corresponding one of gold, recombine them, and you will have gold.' It was equally true and impossible.

 p. 18, l. 562. Cf. Canon's Yeoman's Tale, 16909—13.

 p. 18, l. 570. To 'funny' a person, *i. e.* to mislead them, is a vulgarism sometimes in use in the present day. It is met, I think, somewhere in Albert Smith's books. Such remarks begin to be common in alchemical writings— before this time they were rare.

 p. 18, l. 572. Outragious, l. 650, Pardoner's Tale.

 p. 19, l. 578. A rather poor comparison.

 p. 19, l. 579. Recalls the monastic fish-ponds, of which traces can still be seen near old abbeys.

 p. 19, l. 582. These lines may have been written with the experience of Lydgate's master, and of many others, in view. There can be no doubt that Chaucer had invested money in alchemy—his bitterness shows that—and that

there was a public who knew something of the technicalities of alchemy. The statute forbidding it passed in 1403.
Chaucer's words are similar:

> 'Lo / swich a lucre / is in this lusty game
> A mannes myrthe / it wol turne vn-to grame
> And empten also / grete and heuye purses
> And maken folk / for to purchacen curses.'
> C. Y. Tale. Ellesmere MS., 6-Text, ll. 16870—73.

p. 19, l. 588. C. Y. T. 16925, 'ignotum per ignotius.' I cannot trace this, but it is medieval divinity.

p. 19, l. 594. *Complexiouns.* See l. 1236.

p. 19, l. 603-5. There is no doubt but that either by tradition or by some separate text, perhaps a sidenote, Lydgate had become aware of Johannes Hispalensis' connection with the *Sec. Sec.* He accordingly confuses John, son of Patrick (the Syrian compiler), with John Avendeath (Hispalensis), the translator of part of the treatise for *Teophine.* The headline, p. 20, represents Lydgate's intention. Lydgate begins in the third person, and getting tired, makes an awkward change in l. 622.

p. 20, l. 613. One MS. of the *Sec. Sec.* gives Herodos, others Hermes.

p. 20, l. 637. Misled by this line, the rubricator (? Burgh) has made the following an epistle of the translator. It is really—as far as it is anything—a translation of part of the preface to the *Sec. Sec.* See cap. IV. of the English prose version (18 A. vii., Mus. Brit.).

p. 20, l. 638. Lydgate again begins in the third person, and again changes in 663, this time in a more workman-like manner. The preface begins with an equivalent for l. 655, then excuses himself for not coming (641-51), then remarks on the sin of disclosing secrets, then goes on to ll. 652-6, a summary of the objects of some of the next chapters.

p. 22, ll. 663—679, represent the advice Lydgate thought necessary for Henry VI. and his court.

p. 22, ll. 673-4. A confusion of metaphors, brought on by looking for a metaphor for everything, an instance of the error into which some of our modern poets have fallen.

p. 22, l. 680. 'togidre to combyne' is not here simply half a line put in to make up a rhyme, but seems to come in the sense. Confer version A., cap. IV., where the author speaks of the necessity of keeping the people in subjection.

p. 22, l. 687. Lydgate goes off again on a tangent, with a general idea of the first of the preceding prefaces, and does not return till l. 729.

p. 22, l. 689. 'Discrecion, prudence in right judgemente,
Whiche in a prince is thing most convenable.'
Pallas to Paris of Troie, 26.

p. 22, l. 698. These lines should come in—by sense—after 98.

p. 22, l. 700. *moo,* ? me; very unusual.

p. 22, l. 702. 'above the sterryd hevene,' *ad empireum coelum,* Sec. Sec.

p. 22, l. 703. See l. 87.

p. 22, l. 704. See note on ll. 351—321.

p. 23, l. 709. See l. 112.

p. 23, l. 712. *porrus,* Porus, the Indian king defeated by Alexander.

p. 23, l. 713. *Vows of the peacock* were now a thing of the past.

p. 23, l. 722. Persons used to the precision of German scholarship often PHILOSOPHERS.

speak of the ignorance of Chaucer and Lydgate, to say nothing of other poets, in speaking of Helicon as a spring. In Add. MS. 29729, we have in the Mercer's Play, fol. 132 b, the following lines showing their ideas:

> 'And percius / with his furious stede
> Smot on the roche / wher ye musis dwell
> tyll ther sprange vp / sodenly a well
> Callid the welle / of Calyope
> Moste auctorysyd / amonges thes Cyryens
> Of which the poetes / that dwell in y^t. cuntre
> And othar famous / Rethorycyens
> And they that calid / be musycyens
> Ar wont to drynke / of that holsom welle
> Which y^t. all othar / in vertue dothe exselle.'

fol. 133 a,

The fact that there were springs on the mountain of Helicon, springs haunted by the Muses (for which they had Hesiod's authority), was quite sufficient for any medieval writer.

p. 23, l. 728. There was no fear of Lydgate's revealing anything that was not patent to everybody. One may hope the reader will get some pure corn out of the chaff of these 735 lines.

p. 23, l. 736. 'Reges sunt quattuor: Rex largus sibi et largus subditis: Rex avarus sibi et avarus subditis. Rex avarus sibi, et largus subditis: Rex largus sibi et avarus subditis. Itali ei utique dixerunt: non est vitium in rege: si est avarus sibi et largus-subditis. Indi vero dixerunt: rex avarus sibi et subditis bonus est. Perses vero contrarium afferentes, et contradicentes Indis et Italicis dixerunt nihil valet rex qui non est largus sibi et subditis. Sed inter omnes meo judicio pejor est ille & magis reprobandus qui est largus sibi et avarus subditis, quia regnum illius cito destruetur.'—*Sec. Sec.*

It will be seen Lydgate gets the whole thing wrong as a translation. One of the Latin editions attributed this classification to Pythagoras.

p. 23, l. 738. *with al ther besy cure.*
  'But my entente and al my besie cure.'—*C. of L.* 36.
  'Though all the worlde doe his busy cure.'
   Balade 'warnyng men,' &c., 22.

p. 24, l. 755. This must be put down again as Lydgate's idea of the advice needed by the English court of the day.

p. 25, ll. 789-91. These lines are not clear—in fact Lydgate seems to mean the very opposite of what he says.

p. 25, l. 792. ll. 736—791 apparently are a summary of the chapter on the four manners of kings—and now Lydgate harks back to the beginning again.

p. 26, l. 804. If there were any other authority for the word I would prefer to read 'fredain' from the French, whim, fancy, will, &c. There would be no difference in the MS.

p. 26, l. 814. There is no second extremity mentioned, and the whole stanza is doubled up hopelessly.

p. 26, l. 834. London fogs were as famous as they are now, before coal came there. Cf. 'Of ignoraunce the miste to chace away.'—*C. of L.* 25.

p. 27, l. 838. 'laureer meed of mightie conquerors.'—*Ass. of Foules.*

p. 27, l. 855. Lydgate returns again to the subject of lines 748-56, and this time gets it nearly right.

p. 28, ll. 876-89. Lydgate's own verses—and they shine by comparison with those around them.

p. 28, l. 883. 'That tabouren in your eris many a soun.'
  Leg. G. W. 379, 390.

Notes to Pages 28—31; *Lines* 884—973.

p. 28, l. 884. *The tenour Round.* The tenor bell is the great bell of a peal.
p. 28, l. 887. *Flowers of Proserpina.* The first use of this figure?
p. 28, l. 898. 'discretioun' is object to 'medle.'
p. 29, l. 939. 'But of his owne to large is he that list
Give moche and lesin his gode name therfore.'
B. D. s. M. 455.

p. 30, ll. 942-3. 'Qui vero fundit bona sui regni indignis et non indigentibus: talis est depopulator reipublicae, destructor regni, incompetens reginis: unde prodigus appellatur, eo que procul a regno est sua prudentia. Nomen vero avariciae multum dedecet regem, et disconvenit regiae majestati.'
—*Sec. Sec.*

p. 30, l. 952. *Tressyd as phebus.* The sun's rays spoken of as his hair. A new chapter begins here, which Burgh did not recognize when settling the text.

p. 30, l. 954. *Republica* is Lydgate's own word—not found in the texts.

p. 30, l. 955. *pleyne,* border on, incline to.

p. 30, l. 966. 'Fortem, justum, gravem, magnanimum, largum, beneficum, et liberalem esse, hae sunt regiae laudes.'—Cicero, pro rege Dejot x.

p. 30, l. 966. 'Unde inveni scriptum in preceptis magni doctoris Hermogenis: que summa & mera bonitas: claritas intellectus: et plenitudo legis: ac signum perfectionis est in rege: abstinentia a pecuniis: et possessionibus subditorum. Qua fuit causa destructionis regni Chaldaeorum: &c. &c.'—*Sec. Sec.*

noblesse has the same double meaning as nobility, an abstract and collective noun.

p. 30, l. 973. In many of the French versions there follows a translation of the other part of the chapter, giving an account of the destruction of the English instead of 'angelorum' (MSS.) or 'Chaldaeorum.' See above. It is a heading in the Lambeth MS. 501.

p. 30, ll. 974—1029. These lines are a translation of the chapter 'De lapide animali vegetabili.' As it is short, and not found in one of the texts, I add it. 'In primis O Alexander tibi tradere volo secretorum maximum secretum, et divina potentia juvet te ad perficiendum propositum, et ad celandum ad arcanum. Accipe ergo lapidem animalem vegetabilem et mineralem qui non est lapis, nec habet naturam lapidis, et iste lapis quodam modo assimilatur lapidibus montium minerarum et plantarum et animalium, et reperitur in quolibet loco, et in quolibet tempore, et in quolibet homine: et convertibilis est in quemlibet colorem, et in se continet omnia elementa, et dicitur minor mundus: et ego nominabo ipsum nomine suo, quo nominat ipsum vulgus scilicet terminus ovi, hoc est dicere ovum philosophorum. Divide ergo ipsum in quattuor partes, quaelibet pars habet unam naturam; deinde compone ipsum equaliter et proportionabiliter, itaque non sit in eo divisio nec repugnantia, et habebis propositum, Domino concedente. Isto modo est universalis, sed ego dividam ipsum tibi in operationes speciales: dividitur itaque in quattuor et duobus modis sit bene et sine corruptione. Quando igitur habueris aquam ex aere, et aerem ex igne, et ignem ex terra, tunc habebis plene artem. Dispone ergo substantiam aeream per discretionem, et dispone substantiam terream per humiditatem et caliditatem: donec conveniant et conjungantur sic quae nec dividantur nec discrepent: et tunc adjunge eis duas virtutes operativas, scilicet aquam et ignem: et tunc implebitur opus tuum. Quia si permiscueris aquam solam dealbabit, et si adjunxeris ignem rubescet, Domino concedente.'—*Sec. Sec.*

p. 31, l. 973. One is constantly coming across statements such as the following of the good rulers in Arabic books: 'Qutb-ad-din was generous; he

H 2

governed his people with humanity, treated merchants well, and loaded them with gifts. His subjects lived in the greatest abundance, loaded with his largesse, and fearing no damage from him.'

p. 31, l. 982. *Regent*: note the broader sense in which this word is used.

p. 31, ll. 988—994. This is incorrectly drawn up, and is corrected in the next two lines. The state of the lines in the MS. seems to point that this was the fair copy for presentation, destined to be personally corrected by Burgh.

p. 31, l. 995. The following explanation is given in the *Rosarium Philosophorum*, p. 267. 'Aristoteles in regimine principum dicit ad Alexandrum de quatuor elementis — Quando habueris aquam, id est Mercurium (perhaps mercury; perhaps the "mercury of philosophers") ex aere, id est sole (gold), et aerem ex igne, scilicet spiritum Mercurii (a volatile acrid compound, corrosive sublimate, arsenic, orpiment, or the like), & ignem scilicet mercurium ex terra scilicet luna (silver), tunc plene habebis artem.'

p. 31, l. 999. See note on l. 561.

p. 32, l. 1002. Citron is simply gold coloured, with a purple tinge. 'Quandoque bonus dormitat Homerus'; and Prof. Skeat remarks in a note to his introduction to the *Canon's Yeoman's Tale*, on the strange alchemical scale of colour—black, red, white. This was of course the Aristotelian scale, *Arist. de Sensu et Sensile* ii, *Barth. de Prop. Rerum*, xix. vii, f. 354 a, and all other colours were put somewhere in this scale—white, yellow, citrine, red, purple, green, black. The Arab commentators name sixteen colours, white and black, and two sevens, between red and white or black.

p. 32, ll. 1007-8. These lines represent the last lines of the Latin chapter. Mercury, or any compound of it, would make any metal of a silvery colour by 'amalgamating' its outside, while arsenic, orpiment, &c. might redden it.

p. 32, l. 1008. This verse refers to the traditional connection between the moon and silver.

p. 32, l. 1009. The side-heading was written with the names of some French alchemists in my mind, and I hoped to have identified them, but it seems there was no ground for Lydgate's line—though, of course, Philip of Tripoli may have been French, and may have been an alchemist.

p. 32, l. 1023. 'Et pater noster Hermogenes qui est triplex in philosophia.' *Sec. Sec.* All followers of these mysteries were sons of Hermes. It may not be out of place to mention that Trismegistus does not mean 'thrice great' but thrice greatest, or greatest in three—places, things, sciences, &c.

p. 32, l. 1024. *with seyd Phelip*, with the said Philip. 'Secree' was admitted to his confidence.

p. 32, l. 1025. *prevy* would be the attribute of 'vertu,' I suppose. There is a chapter in the Latin text on the virtues of stones (but see the Lambeth text), 'with circumstances of Araby, Ind, & Perse.'

p. 32, l. 1030. This stanza represents the chapter 'de intentione finali quem debent habere reges.' It is probable that in this, as in many later sections, Lydgate made a kind of skeleton, beginning to translate a chapter, and letting the one stanza stand for the whole, which later on would be finished. Very difficult to scan.

p. 33, l. 1037. This stanza stands for the chapter, 'De malis quae sequuntur ex carnali appetitu.'

p. 33, ll. 1051-78 represent the chapter, 'De sapientia regis et religione.' Book II. begins here.

p. 33, l. 1060. It is very noteworthy that nothing at all is said in any text about tale-bearers, and yet Lydgate returns to the point again and again. Had he in mind the condition of the English court? There is no doubt that 'no wit of sapience or of discretion' could have been found in Henry VI. judged by this rule, and Benedict Burgh, who supplied the headings, and was connected with a Yorkist family, may have wished to bring this prominently forward. I may say that when the title of the section is in the margin, it is so simply for convenience, and its position implies nothing else.

p. 34, l. 1065. The title would again point to Henry—more favourably this time. The stanzas have no authority in the text, and are wholly Lydgate's. Cf. XI. of the A.-text.

p. 34, l. 1079. This is the chapter 'de ornamento regis.' Lydgate makes no use of the text before him.

p. 34, l. 1085. 'Saphirus is a precious stone, & is blew in colour / mooste like to heven in faire wether & clere, & is best amonge precious stones / & most precious & most apte & able to fyngres of kinges... And this saphire stone is thick and not passing bright, as Isid. saith... Also in Lapidario hit is sayde / that this stone doth awaye ennye, and putteth of dred & feare, & maketh a man bold & hardy, & master and victor, & maketh the harte stedfast in goodnes / and maketh meke and milde, & goodly. I wene that al this is said more in disposition than in effecte & doyng. But this suffyseth at this tyme.'—*Barth. Angl. de Prop. Reb.*, XVI. lxxxvii. f. 337, Ed. 1535. I don't know whether Lydgate meant that a sapphire was always of one hue, for medieval writers made it a great point that if the wearer of a sapphire lost his chastity, the sapphire lost its colour... Alesius of Piedmont in his *Secrets. Bas.*, 8°., f. 746, says that the sapphire easily loses its colour by fire. But perhaps Lydgate only referred to its hardness.

p. 34, l. 1086. Here two chapters of the text are omitted; see the A.-text. This chapter is 'de castitate.' It urges him to be chaste, so that he does not resemble swine. The original referred to that vice, 'not so much as to be named among Christian men,' as Blackstone says.

p. 34, l. 1091. *Pallith*. The sense here is midway between the active meaning of beat and the passive of becoming vapid, and includes part of both.

p. 35, l. 1093. In the Arabic *Prairies d'Or* (tr. B. de Meynard) I find: 'Dans l'Inde, un roi ... ne se montre au peuple qu'à des époques déterminées, et seulement pour examiner les affaires de l'etat: car, dans leur idées, un roi porterait atteinte à sa dignité et n'inspirerait plus le même respect s'il se montrait constamment au peuple.'

p. 35, l. 1093. This is a part of a previously omitted chapter, 'de taciturnitate regis': the point of that chapter being advice to a king to show himself to his subjects not more than once or twice a year. This is fortified by a reference to the kingdom of the Indians, which our A.-prose turns into Jews as usual, and which Lydgate, or the text he used, turns into Rome, as an example more likely to be followed than that of the Jews.

p. 35, l. 1099. *yerde*. The rod has been the symbol of authority from the time of the writer of Genesis to our own. The connection between the yard and the rod of 5½ yards, recognised as far back as Ed. 1.'s time legally, would be an interesting study.

Vndir a yerde.
      'Shewe forthe the yerde of castigacion.'—*Stedfastnesse* 26.
      'Undir your yerde egall to mine offence.'—*T. & C.*, iii. 137.
      'And mekely take her chastisement and yerde.'—*C. of L.* 363.

p. 35, l. 1103. *daungeer*. Distrust, a character in the *Romance of the Rose*.

p. 35, l. 1107. The title of these stanzas seems to have been suggested by line 1106: but there is no reason in the texts for making a new heading. All other MSS. put this heading here. It might have been better to leave it out altogether.

p. 36, l. 1121. This chapter is headed, 'de solatio musicali regis.' It advises the king to make all his intimates drunk two or three times a year to hear what their private thoughts of him and his government are.

p. 36, l. 1126. Lydgate throws in this sentiment, entirely opposed to the texts, to conciliate the commoners of England. See the A.-prose for the real sentiment.

p. 36, l. 1128. This heading also is not an original division of the text, which runs on.

p. 36, l. 1130. The memory of the king who encourages it.

p. 36, l. 1135. . This is part of the chapter 'In quibus consistit obedientia Domini.' 'O Alexander, obedienta dominatoris quatuor attenditur modis, in religiositate, in dilectione, in curialitate, et reverentia.' *Sec. Sec.* It will be seen that our author only began the idea and did not finish it.

p. 36, l. 1140. *seyn* = seen.
'For they han seyn hir euer so vertuous.'—*M. of Law Tale* 624.
'And whan they han this blisful mayden seyn.'—*M. of Law Tale* 172.

p. 36, l. 1142. This heading seems to have been put on the scrap of paper on which Burgh found stanzas 164 and 165. These stanzas are a part of the same chapter as the preceding one, and have no reference to how a king should be governed in different weathers, but, instead, compare the government of a king to the weather, which does good or harm to the people without their having much to say in the matter.

p. 37, l. 1154. Our author's conclusion is his own, and is much better than that of the texts, which advise the subjects 'to grin & bear it.'

p. 37, l. 1156. This represents the chapter 'de misericordia regis.' It is again merely a stanza to represent what Lydgate doubtless intended to fill in later.

Between this and the next stanza come two chapters, one advising the king to store up grain against famine time, and then to sell it to the people; the other speaking of God's revenge against man-slaying—even by a king. The first would have led at once to the dethronement of any English king, let alone the fact that Henry's government never had any money, and the second would have been peculiarly unacceptable to the nobles of that day.

p. 37, l. 1163. This represents the chapter 'de fide servanda.' It is again a skeleton battalion.

p. 37, l. 1164. The reference here is to the centre of the universe—but why in one degree? I suppose Lydgate got 'mutabylite' and filled in the other two rhymes till he could get a better one, We must remember that he did not publish this.

p. 37, l. 1170. This stands for 'Quomodo Rex debet ordinare studia.' The text of the *Sec. Sec.* dates from before universities, and so one could hardly expect to find them mentioned in it. The Latin text begins 'Prepara gymnasia.' The whole of this section is Lydgate's, the idea only being supplied by the *Sec. Sec.* See notes on l. 341.

p. 38, l. 1184. This is part of the chapter 'de hora eligendi in Astronomia.' The next hundred lines however do not follow the *Sec. Sec.* at all closely, or more properly do not translate it at all.

p. 38, l. 1189. *Cypryan.* Where did Lydgate get Cypryan from? Was this the St. Cyprian who was an astrologer at Antioch, who afterwards became a Bishop, and was martyred in the Dioclesian persecution? The French and Latin texts at this place speak of *Plato* as referring the evils our bodies suffer from, to four contrary humours. See note on l. 1240. Lydgate quotes Cyprian, 'A garden of his flowers.' See p. 80, *Eliz. Acad.*, E. E. T. S.

Notes to Page 38; Lines 1191—1207.

p. 38, l. 1191. This seems to be founded on some lines at the end of the chapter on studies. Speaking of the Greeks, he says, 'Sane puellae in domo patris familias ex magno studio sciebant cursum anni, festa futura, solemnitates mensium, cursus planetarum, causas abreviatorias diei et noctis, revolutionem pleiadis et bootes, circulum dierum, signa stellarum, judicia futurorum, & alia quae pertinent ad artem superiorum.'—*Sec. Sec.*

p. 38, l. 1198. 'O Rex clementissime, si fieri potest nec surgas, nec sedeas, nec comedas, nec bibas, nec penitus aliquid facias, sine consilio periti in astrorum arte.'—*Sec. Sec.*

p. 38, l. 1203 same rhyme as 1231-2.

p. 38, l. 1205. This is not in the *Sec. Sec.*, nor is it justified by the science of the time. I should prefer to read the line,

'Saturn is slouhe and malencolyous.'

And when we remember that we are dealing with fragments only we may feel ourselves free to omit Mars from the list. The following lines are from Harl. 2251, 23 b:

'Saturne disposithe / to malencoly
Iupiter reysethe men / to hye noblesse
Sturdy Mars / to stryfe werre and envye
Phebus to wisdom / and to highe prowesse
Mercury to chaunge / and doublenesse
The moone makithe man / mutable and mevynge
How shulde man thanne / be stable of livynge.'

'As Ptholomeus sayth in libro de judiciis Astrorum, he maketh a man broun and fowle, mysdoynge, slowe and heuy eleynge and sory / seldome gladde and merye or laughynge / and therfore Ptholomeus saith, they that ben subject to Saturnus, haue oft euyl drye chinnes in the hynder part of the fote. And ben yelowe of colour, and broun of heere / and sharpe in all the body, and vnsemely. And ben not skoymous of foul and stynkyng clothynge. And he loveth stynkyng beestes and vnclene / soure thynges and sharp. For of theyr complexyon Melancolyke humour hath maystry.'—*Barth. Ang. de Prop. Rerum.* VIII. xxiii, fol. 126 b., Ed. 1535. See also *Bapt. Porta. Coelestis Physiog.*, II. cap. 1, 4, 6, 7.

But.—
'O cruell Mars, full of Melancoly,
And of thy kind, hote, combust & dry.'
Story of Thebes iii. 1.

'Mars malencolyous.' I think it better here to add the notes about the disposition of Mars from the same source.

'And he dysposeth the soule to vnstedfaste wytte and lyghtnes / to wrathe, and to boldnes, and to other coleryke passyons. And also he dysposethe and makethe able to fyrye werkes and craftes, as smythes and bakers, as Saturnus dysposeth men to be erthe tyllars, and berers of heuy bourdens. And Jupiter the contrarye disposeth to lyght craftes: for he maketh men able to be pleders / chaungers, handlers of syluer, wryters / and other suche / as Misaelle (*Messahala*) sayth. Ca. xii.'—*B. A.* VIII. xxv. See also *Porta lib. cit.* c. 15—21.

p. 38, l. 1206. But Lydgate elsewhere says,

'And phebus Causith / dysposyng to gladnesse.'

'Also among all planetes he disposethe most beastes to boldnesse and to lyuelynesse.'—*B. A.* VIII. xxviii.

p. 38, l. 1207. 'In Rethoryk / helpith mercuryvs.'

'Fore Mercuriales cordatos, ingeniosos, cuncta discentes, modestos, mercatores, Grammaticos, Oratores, Physicos, Poetas, Musicos, Mathematicos, sortilegos, augures.'—*Porta lib. cit.* c. 18.

'Vnder Mercurius is conteined fortune, chaffering, & yeft: & he tokeneth wysdom & wyt.'—*B. A.* VIII. xxvii.

> 'With boke in hand than comes Mercurious
> Right eloquent and ful of rethoric
> With polite termis and delicious
> With penne and inke to report alredie
> Sething songis & singing merily.
> IIis hode was red heclid altour his croun
> Like til a poete of the olde fassioun.'
> *Test. of Cres.* 239; *T. of Glas* 132.

p. 39, l. 1208. 'as Ptholomeus saythe, the moone maketh a man vnstable, chaungeable, and remeuynge aboute fro place to place.'—*B. A.* VIII. xxx. 'item homines nullius utilitatis, qui die ac nocte desiderent ire huc illuc, nec leviter alicubi stent, instabiles, non perseverantes, habentes ex operibus legationes, aquarum et terrae amantes, voraces, extra patriam viventes,' &c.— *Porta,* c. 45-9.

p. 39, l. 1212. This title has nothing to do with the stanza, which does not seem to be more than a collection of clauses.

p. 39, l. 1222. *the* = thee.

p. 39, l. 1223. *word is but wind.*

> 'What availeth, sir, your proclamacion
> of curious talking, not touching sadnes?
> It is but winde.'—*Craft of Lovers,* 37.

'Worde is but wind brought in by enuye.'—*Falls of Princes* 216, and in *Troy-Book. Temple of Glas* 1183, which see for further references.

p. 39, l. 1226. These two stanzas really should come after the next section, of which they form a part.

p. 40, l. 1236. 'Complexioun.' The following lines are from Harl. 2251, 23 *b*:

> 'The sangwyne man / of bloode hathe hardynesse
>   Made to be louynge / and large of expence
> The flewmatyke slowe / oppressede withe dulnesse
>   White of coloure / rude of eloquence
>   And sithe there is in man / suche difference
>   Of complexions / diuersely tournynge
>   How shulde man thanne / be stable in his livynge.
>
> The coleryke man sotyl / and disceyvable
>   Sklondre lene / and cytryne of coloure
> Wrothe sodainly / and hastily vengeable
>   ffrette withe Ire / withe fury and withe rancour
>   Drye and aduste / and a grete wastour
>   And disposede to many a sundry thynge
>   How shulde he thanne / be stable in livenge.
>
> Malencolicus / of his complexioune
>   Disposede is / for to be fraudulent
> Malicious frowarde / and be decepcioune
>   Conspirynge discorde / ay double of his entente
>   Whiche thynges peysede / by goode avisemente
>   I dare conclude / as to my felynge
>   ffewe men ben stable here / in theyr livynge.'

There are four complexions : sanguine, choleric, melancholic, and phlegmatic, answering to the four humours, 'sanguis, cholera, phlegma, melancholia.'

p. 40, l. 1240. 'Conveniunt itaque sapientes et philosophi naturales : *quod homo est compositus ex oppositis elementis : et ex quatuor contrariis humoribus : qui semper indigent alimentis et potibus : quibus si caret homo corrumpitur eius su[b]stantia : et si his superflue vtatur : vel diminute incurrit debilitatem et infirmitatem et alia inconvenientia multa. Si vero vtitur temperate : inveniet iuuamen vitae corporis fortitudinem, et totius suae substantiae salutem.'—Sec. Sec.*

p. 40, l. 1241. 'Humorum autem genera quattuor sunt, sic sanguis, colera, flegma, et melencolia.'—*Arnoldus Villanovanus, Spec. Introd. Med.* cap. iiii. (*Op. Lugd.* 1520, fo. 2ª.).

'Nam cum quatuor illa sint, ex quibus compactum est corpus, Terra, Ignis, Aqua, Aer, horum contra naturam abundantia, defectusque, et ex loco proprio in alienum translatio, per quam quod sibi conveniens est, non tenent, intestinam quandam seditionem et morbos inferunt.'—*Plato in Timaeo*, 1081, d. Ed. Francft. fo. 1602.

'Prima statui potest ea, quae ex primordiis conficitur, iis, quae nonnulli elementa appellant, terram dico, aerem, aquam, ignem : sed melius fortasse dici potest, ex virtutibus confici elementorum, iisque non omnibus : humiditas enim et siccitas, et caliditas et frigiditas, materia corporum sunt compositorum.'—*Arist. de part. anim.* II. i. Ed. Paris 1524, f. 6 b.

p. 40, l. 1244. *tours*—turnings, courses of the planets, whether their movement be direct or retrograde. Their governance in heaven causes temperate health on earth.

p. 40, l. 1246. 'in corporibus medicus sanitatem non internecione caloris aut frigoris, sed proportione quaerit atque conficit.'—*Plut. de Sanit. tuenda.*

p. 40, l. 1247. *Corrupcioun* means a change, not necessarily implying our meaning. Thus when we set a stick on fire we *corrupt* the wood and generate fire.

p. 40, l. 1254. Cicero ad. fam. 16: 'Valetudinem postulare concoctionem, jucunditatem, deambulationem moderatam, delectationem, purgationem ventris.' The ancients summed up the points of diet in the 'six non-naturals'— air, exercise and rest, food and drink, sleep and watching, swiving, and accidents of the mind.

p. 40, l. 1254. This should be called, 'What a Leech has to do.' The next seven stanzas seem to have little to do with the *Sec. Sec.* They express generally some ideas in it, but Lydgate alters very much both the form and the subject matter of the work. They correspond closely to the *Dietary.*

p. 40, ll. 1258-60. Connection of seasons and humours : flewm in autumn, see l. 1413 ; colera in summer, l. 1349. The following lines are taken from Harl. 2251, 23 *a* :

'With veer man hathe / hete and eke moysture
  Atwene bothe / by a maner attemperaunce
In whiche tweyne / grete luste he dothe recure
If colde nat put hym / in distemperaunce
Thus meynte with drede / is manne gouernaunce
  Ay neuer in certeyne / by recorde of writynge
  How shulde he thanne / be stable in livynge.

Man hath with somer / dryenesse and heete
  In theyre bookes / as auctours liste expresse

And whanne phebus / entrithe the Aryete
Digeste humours / vpwarde don hem dresse
Pooris opyn / that season of swetnesse
And exalacions / diuersely wirkynge
How shulde a man / be stable in his livynge.
Autumpne to veer / is founde contrarye
As Galyen saithe / in al his qualitees
Disposynge man / that seasons dothe so vary
To many vnkouthe / straunge Infirmytees
Of canyculer dayes / takynge the propirtees
By reuoluciouṇe / of manyfolde chaungynge
How shulde man thanne / be stable in lyvenge.
Man hathe withe wynter / in this presente lyfe
By disposicioune / colde and humydite
Whiche season is / to fleawme nutritife
Spoylithe tree and herbe / of al theyre fresshe beaute
Closithe, constreynethe / the poores men may see
Causithe kyndely hete / inwarde to be werkynge
How shal man thanne / be stable in his livynge.'

p. 40, l. 1261. *Sleep nurse of digestion.* Chaucer, *Sq. Tale*, 2nd part, l. 1.

'Haec eadem cibus, in venas dum diditur omnes,
Efficit, et multo sopor ille gravissimus exstat,
Quem satur aut lassus capias: quia plurima tum se
Corpora conturbant magno concussa labore.'
Lucretius, IV. 952; see l. 1892.

'The ancient rule was to put a little exercise between a meal and sleep.'—*Plutarch de Is. et Os.*

'Nos autem medicis pareamus, qui monent semper inter coenam et somnum faciendam aliquam intercapedinem : ne congestis in corpus cibis et oppresso spiritu, confestim crudo ac fervido alimento aggravemus vim concoctricem, sed respirationem & relaxationem concedamus.'—*Plut. de Sanit. tuenda*, fo. 133, d.

p. 41, l. 1267. 'And vse neuer late / for to suppe.'
'Suffre no surfetis.'—*Dietary* 8.

p. 41, ll. 1268-70.
'in omni vita certissime precipitur ut perturbationes fugiamus.'—*Cicero Off.* I. 38.

'Quando anima corpore admodum potentior est exultat in eo atque effectur, totum ipsum intrinsecus quatiens languoribus implet.'—*Plato in Timaeo.*

p. 41, l. 1268. 'Si vis incolumen, si vis te reddere sanum
Curas tolle graves, irasci crede prophanum
Parce mero, cenato parum.'—*Schola Salernitana* (11th cent.).

'Pars animam laqueo claudunt mortisque timorem
Morte fugant, ultroquo vocant venientia fata.'—*Ovid*, 7 Met.

p. 41. l. 1271. 'Aer sit mundus, habitabilis, ac luminosus,
Nec sit infectus nec olens fetor cloacae.'—*Schol. Salern.*

p. 41, l. 1274. 'Flee mystis blake / and eyre of pestilence.'—*Dietary.*

p. 41, l. 1275.
'Si tibi deficiant medici; medici tibi fiant
Haec tria: mens laeta, requies, moderata dieta.'—*Schol. Salern.*

p. 41, l. 1278. In this stanza the only change from the *Dietary* beyond the omission of the seventh line is the substitution of 'malencolyous' for 'malicious' in the Harl. 2251 ed., which is much nearer the Latin text of Sl. 3534 than the Lamb. MS.

Notes to Pages 41—43; Lines 1282—1345.

p. 41, l. 1282. This is the eighth stanza in the Harl. 2251 and in the Latin Dietary. It is not included in the *Babee's Book* text.

p. 41, l. 1289. This stanza is in both dietaries, with the exception of the two last lines.

p. 41, l. 1294. Lydgate evidently thought that if these precepts were not in the *Sec. Sec.* they were useful to his patron, and so runs in the old stanzas with this tag. Note the change of meaning in 'diet.'

p. 42, l. 1303. Spring begins when the sun enters Aries. This generally happens after mid-day, March 20th. In Lydgate's time the equinox fell earlier owing to the faults of the Julian Calendar. See the notes on the prose versions at this place. Their dates are not Arabic, but are due to Johannes Hispalensis.

'Spryngynge tyme is begynnynge of the yere, that begynnethe whar the son is in the fyrste party of the sygne that hyghte Aries : and begynnethe to passe vpwarde, toward the Northe by a ryght line, as Constantine saith in Pantegni libro quinto, capitulo tertio.'—*Bart. Angl.* IX. v.

p. 42, l. 1304. The sun now crosses the line, and every day becomes higher at noontide.

p. 42, l. 1305. The daisy opens now as early as the 9th of February. Alceste was turned into a daisy. See Skeat's note in *Legend of Good Women*.

'And aldernext was þe fressh quene
I mene Alceste, the noble trw wyfe,
And for Admete how she lost hir life,
And for hir trouth, if I shal not lie,
Hou she was turnyd to a daisie.'—*T. of Glas* 70-4.

p. 42, l. 1310. 'Ver est calidum et humidum et temperatum : aeri simile est, et excitatur in eo sanguis.'—*Sec. Sec.*

'And spryngnge tyme is betwene hotte and colde / most temperat bitwene winter and somer / meane in qualyte : and partyneth with eyther of them in qualyte.'—*Bart. Angl. loc. cit.*

This last is derived from Galen. Hippocrates said the qualities of spring were warm and moist, and thus it resembles the element air. The Latin text combines both ideas.

p. 42, l. 1322. I cannot find out what story is here alluded to. The cuckoo is, of course, a migratory bird, which stays with us from April to August, and his note is a love-call peculiar to the male and to the nesting season.

p. 43, l. 1334. 'hau' should be 'han'; perhaps ou[r] is on = one talent out of four entrusted to us.

'not onely my daies but fivefold talent.'—*Rem. of Love* 89.

p. 43, l. 1344. Complexion of summer.

'Then somer is hotte and drye / and bredeth Coleram.'—*Bar. Angl.* IX. vi.

p. 43, l. 1345. 'Aestas tunc incipit cum sol ingreditur primum punctus Cancri & continet nonaginta duos dies et horam cum dimidia : et hoc est a decima die junii usque ad decimam diem septembris.'—*Sec. Sec.*

The summer signs are Cancer, Leo, and Virgo.

'And somer hathe thre monthes ryght as spryngyng tyme / as Constantyne sayth. The fyrste monthe longeth to the sygne that hyght Cancer / and lasteth fro the xvij daye of June to the eyghtyne daye of July : The seconde whan the sonne is in Leone, and dureth from the xviij daye of July to the xvij daye of Auguste : The thyrde begynneth whan the sonne commeth in to the sygne that hyghte Virgo, and dureth fro the xvij daye of Auguste to the xviij daye of Septembre, as Constantyne sayth.'—*Barth. Angl.* IX. vi.

Summer now begins about midday on June 21st, and lasts to midnight on September 22nd. St. Barnabas Day is June 11th.

p. 43, l. 1348. See l. 1344.

'Haec anni pars acutis morbis et biliosis est obnoxia, propter aestus bilem generantis vehementiam.'—*Wendelin Cont. Physic. Camb.* 1648, 4° p. 605.

p. 43, l. 1351. St. Bartholomew is August 24th.

p. 43, l. 1352. 'Colour'? Choler, or it may be that Clour is in apposition to Fire as Juventus to Age. For 'Juventus' read 'Iuventus.'

p. 43, l. 1354:

'Est et humor colerae qui competit impetuosis,
Hoc genus est hominum cupiens precellere cunctos.
Hi leviter discunt : multum comedunt : cito crescunt.
Inde magnanimi sunt largi summa petentes.
Hirsutus : fallax : irascens : prodigus : audax :
Astutus : gracilis : siccus : croceique coloris.'—*Schol. Salern.*

p. 43, l. 1356. *Of growing slaundre*, slender of growth. The other MSS. read 'slaundre,' and as this does not follow the *Sec. Sec.*, I decided to follow their spelling. It means 'slender,' as the following extract shows :—

'And the werkynge of somer by subtyltye of heate, cometh in to the holow parties of beestes, and dryeth and wasteth humours / that bene bytwene the skynne and the fleshe: and all to sheddyth theym, and maketh beestes swyfte : and so he distroyeth and wastyth superfluyte.'—*Bart. Angl.*

p. 44, l. 1361. June 24th is St. John the Baptist's day; June 29th is St. Peter and St. Paul ; August 1st is Lammas Day, St. Peter ad Vincula, when he was released from prison by an angel, and the guards were crucified for letting him go. St. Thomas à Becket was martyred on December 29th, but the time of the year being inconvenient for pilgrims, his bones were 'translated' to a new shrine in summer, and the anniversary was kept as his.

p. 44, ll. 1374-6. Beans and peas, purslane, and lettuce. These are not mentioned in the *Sec. Sec.* (see the prose version).

p. 45, l. 1395. *tydy man.*

'For all the trauayle of the yere is then mooste : and corn & fruytes ben gadered and brought into bernes.'—*Bart. Angl.* IX. vii.

One may be excused for thinking some of these stanzas really good.

p. 45, l. 1405. 'Harueste begynneth, whanne the sonne entryth and cometh in to the fyrste partye of the sygne, that hyght Libra : whan the sonne is in the ryghte lyne that hyght linea equinoctialis : for he is like ferre fro the North, and fro the South. Harueste tyme hath thre monthes, that serue it as Constantyne sayth. The fyrste begynneth, whan the sonne is in Libra : and lastyth fro the xvij daye of Septembre, to the xviij daye of Octobre : and than the sonne begynneth to withdrawe in the myd daye. The seconde month is / in whiche the sonne is in Scorpione : & lastyth fro the xvij. day of Octobre to the eyghtenth day of Nouembre. The thyrde month is, whan the sonne is in Sagittario : and lasteth fro the xvij (*sic*) daye of Nouembre, to the xviij daye of Decembre, as Constantyne sayth.'—*Bart. Angl. loc. cit.*

p. 45, l. 1407. 'Harueste in his qualyte is contrarye to spryngynge tyme : & therfore that time bredeth many euyll syknesses. Galen sayth that Harueste is more pestilencyall than other tymes, and more euyl in many thinges. Fyrst for chaungyng of tyme : for now he is hote, *and* now he is colde / also for he comyth after somer / and findeth many hote humors / that ben full hote / bicause of hete that was in somer : & the colde of harueste smyteth ayen suche humours to the inner partyes : & suffre not them to passe out of the bodyes. And so such humours rotte and brede full euyll sykenesses / & Quartayns / & Feuers that vneth ben curable.'—*Bart. Angl.*

p. 45, l. 1414. 'Autumno morbi accidunt acutissimi & funestissimi ferè.'—*Hippocrat. Aphor.*

p. 45, l. 1415. Autumn is cold and dry, which are the qualities of the element earth.

p. 46, l. 1422. St. Clement's Day, Nov. 23rd.

p. 46, l. 1425. 'unwar' is put in before 'seknessys' in some MSS.

p. 46, l. 1433. This seems to be the only personal note in the poem, and would rather point to an elderly patron.

p. 46, l. 1440. Martinmas is Nov. 11th. This stanza belongs to autumn, and not to this section at all.

p. 46, l. 1448. 'Wynter hyghte Hyems, and hath that name of Eundo, goynge other passynge: For in wynter tyme the sonne treuleth *and* passeth ofter in a shorter cercle than in somer tyme. And therfore he maketh shorter dayes & lenger nightes, as Isydore sayth. And as Constantin saith, wynter begynnoth, whan the sonne is in the sygne that hyghte Capricornus: and is ende of the descencyon and the lowyng of the sonne in the middaye. And then begynneth lytel & lytel to passe vpwarde agaynste the northe. Also wynter hath thre monthes that serue hym. The fyrste begynneth in Capricorne / and lastethe from the eightenthe daye of Decembre / vnto the seuententh daye of Januarii: The seconde is whan the son is in Aquario, and lasteth from 'the seuententh day of Januarii / to the syxtenth day of Feuerer: The thyrde month is / whan the sonne is in the sygne / that hyghte Piscis, and lasteth from the syxtenth day of Februarii / to the eyghtenth daye of Marche. And wynter is colde and moyste / and nouryshethe flewme."—*Bart. Angl.* IX. viii.

p. 48, l. 1491. This line is one of those coincidences which look like design. I do not know that Lydgate's epitaph has been printed lately, so here it is:

'Mortuus seclo superis superstes,
Hac jacet Lidgat tumulatus urna,
Qui fuit quondam celebra Brittanniae
    fama Poesis.'

p. 48, l. 1495. *My lord.* One would like to have had some more personal note than this, but we may feel moderately certain that 'my lord' was Earl Bourchier.

p. 48, l. 1498. Was Burgh one of the 'masters in grammar' who were made at that time? They had not taken a degree, but were examined in Latin grammar and their power of flogging, and then granted a diploma. In that case he would not have made the acquaintance of the seven arts he commemorates in this introduction.

p. 48, l. 1506. The Anticlaudian of Alanus de Insulis is one of the important books of medieval times. It deals with the perfect man warring against vices. Claudian had made a poem where the vicious Rufinus had opposed Stilico: Alanus, to oppose, named his poem the Anti-Claudian. It consists of nine books, and may be read in the Rolls Series in the second series of *Anglo-Latin Satirical Poets*, ed. Wright. London, 1872, or in Migne, t. 210. We may briefly summarize it thus.

Nature, perceiving its failure in bringing about perfection, decides to join in one being all the virtues and excellences possible. She therefore summons all these allegorical personages, and lays before them her plan. Prudence (Phronesis) and Reason remark that none of them can give to man the highest of all gifts—a soul, and that they must ask it from God. This mission is imposed on them, they at first refuse it, but Concord gets them to accept it. A car is made for them by the seven liberal arts, to which five horses representing the senses are yoked. Grammar lays the framework, Logic makes the axles of the wheels, Rhetoric adorns the frame with gems and flowers of silver, Arithmetic, Music, Geometry, and Astronomy make the wheels, and Reason drives the chariot.

They pass through the air, the clouds, the home of the evil spirits of the air, the spheres of the planets, and arrive at the firmament, when Reason faints, and the senses become useless. Theology appears, and on the condition that Reason and the senses—except that of hearing—are abandoned, offers to guide Phronesis. The firmament, the empyrean heavens, the dwellings of saints, angels, and the Mother of God are next described. Here Prudence faints, but Faith revives her, and explains the mysteries of human destiny, grace, &c.

God now orders Intelligence to frame a model of a soul such as was asked for, and making it, it is sent to Nature, who makes a body which Harmony, Music, and Arithmetic fit for and join to the soul. All the allegorical divinities add a gift—even Nobility and Fortune bring theirs—which Wisdom checks and moderates.

But Hell learning of this new creation resolves to destroy it, and Allecto unites all the vices against it. After a long battle the new man puts them all to flight, and inaugurates upon the earth the reign of Justice and Happiness.

p. 49, l. 1536. Repeated later as l. 2191.

p. 49. l. 1541. Fronescis is mother of Philology, in Martianus Capella's *Marriage of Philology and Mercury*, II. 114, IX. 893.

p. 49, l. 1541. See l. 224.

p. 49, l. 1542. In the Anticlaudian, Rhetoric is described as carving and adorning the car of Phronestis with flowers and with inlaid work of silver.

p. 49, l. 1543. Who is this Petir? Burgh knew that Petrarch (1304—1374) was called Francis. (See his ballad in the Introduction.) Petrarch wrote some declamations which were regarded as models of rhetoric in the middle age.

p. 50, l. 1558. This might refer to a royal command, but most probably is a flattery of the Bourchiers, just as the first poem in the *Babee's Book* was written for noble, not for royal children. May that poem not have been written by Burgh?

p. 50, l. 1565. Allecto is the head of the infernal army raised against the perfect man in the Anticlaudian.

p. 51, l. 1608. 'Aqua and vino si misceatur, prodest: et quae inter diluti usum bibitur, ipsum dilutum reddit minus noxium.'—*Plutarch de Sanit. tuenda.* ed. Franc. 1620, f. 132.

p. 51, l. 1609. Water Alchymyn is prepared from Cumin.

p. 51, l. 1611. A side-note in Harl. 2251, quotes from Horace

'Et gravi
Malvae salubres corpori.'—*Ep.* 2. 48.

'Utere lactucis et mollibus utere malvis.'—Mart., 3. 87.

p. 52, l. 1615. This is recommended by Hippocrates. In the prose editions I hope to investigate the relationship between this work and the schools of Arab and Greek medicine.

p. 52, l. 1625. Cf. lines 1268-70.

p. 52, l. 1638. The same thought as in l. 1248.

p. 53, l. 1648. This refers to sulphur baths. 'Balnea sulfureae aquae intrare.'—*Sec. Sec.*

p. 53, l. 1653. 'Regula Hippocratis est: si quis repletus vel constipatus balneum intrabit: ille dolorem vel intestinorum certissime incurrere potest. Si quis coiverit ventre repleto, paralisim incurret. Nec post cibum quis currat vel equitet nimium. Qui simul lac and pisces sepe comedunt, leprum incurrunt. Vinum et lac similia operantur.'—*Sec. Sec.*

p. 53, l. 1655. 'Rhasis discommends all fish, and says they breed viscosities, slimy nutriment, little and humourous nourishment.'—Burton, *Anat. of Mel.*, Part I. ii., 2. 1.

p. 53, l. 1660. This is the beginning of the letter of Diocles (pp. 109-12, Paulus Aeginetus, *Op. Med.* Lugd., 1589. 8vo.). It is practically identical with one written by Antonius Musa (physician to the Emperor Augustus) to Maecenas. The letter was a favourite of our early English ancestors. See a copy in *Leechdoms*, &c.

p. 53, l. 1661. 'Hominis corpus in quatuor parteis diducimus, caput scilicet, thoracem, ventrem, et vesicam.'—*Diocles.*

p. 53, l. 1669. 'Powrys Organycall' is the Virtus Animalis of medieval writers.

p. 53, l. 1670. 'The brayne ... is distingued and departed in thre celles or dennes: ... whiche physytiens calle Ventriculos, small wombes. In the formeste celle and wombe imagination is conformed and made, in the midle, reason, in the hyndermeste, recordation and minde. ... For in the fyrste, shappe and lykenesse of thynges that ben felte, is gendered in the fantasie or in the imagination. Than the shap and lyknesse is sende to the mydell celle, and there ben domes made. And at the laste after dome of reson, that shappe and lyknesse is sende into the celle and wombe of Puppis, and betake to the vertue of mynde.'—*Bart. Angl. de rerum propr., lib.* v. 3, f. 35.

p. 54, l. 1678. 'Quando ergo congregantur superfluitates poteris scire per haec signa, quae sunt; tenebrositas oculorum; gravitas superciliorum, repercussiones temporum; tremitus aurium, inclusio narium.'—*Sec. Sec.*

'Vertigo, capitis dolor, superciliorum gravitas; aures sonant, tempora saliunt, oculi mane illacrymant, caligantque, nares oppletae odorem non sentiunt, dentium gingiuae attolluntur.'—*Diocles.*

'Cum a capite morbus oritur, solet capitis dolor tentari, tunc supercilia gravantur, tempora saliunt, aures sonant, oculi lachrymantur, nares repletae odorem non sentiunt.'—*Ant. Musa ad Maecen.* Nor. 4vo., 1538.

p. 54, l. 1682. 'Aloes,' wormwode (18 A. vij.), 'effeentim, that is Eufrasy' (Lamb. 501), foenci, herbam perforatam (Latin versions), aloyne (Harl. 219, French).

p. 54, l. 1683. 'Dowset and swet wyn.' 'In vino dulci.'—*Sec. Sec.*

p. 54, l. 1685. 'Pulgichyn.' Pulegium, pennyroyal, pudding grass.

p. 54, l. 1687. 'Quum ergo ex his aliquod accidit caput purgari oportet, nullo quidem medicamento, sed vel hyssopi, vel origani summitatibus tritis, quae in ollula cum musto, aut sapae heminae dimidio deferbuerint, atque hoc absorbens jejunus os colluet, et gargarizando humores ex alto deducet,' &c.—*Diocles.*

'Hyssopi autem coronae bubulae fasciculum deferre facies, inde aquam ore continebis, tum caput calide habueris, ut fluat pituita.'—*Ant. Musa ad Maecen.*

p. 54, l. 1696. 'Et utatur in cibo suo grano sinapis.'—*Sec. Sec.*

'Optime facit etiam, si sinapi mulsa calida dilutum jejunus absorbens gargarizet, pituitamque ex capite eliciat.'—*Diocles.*

p. 54, l. 1706.—'Tounge lettyd.' 'Lingua fit ponderosa: os salsum: in orificio cibum acerbum sentit; ac dolorem tussis.'—*Sec. Sec.*

112   *Notes to Pages* 55, 56; *Lines* 1711—1758.

'Cum autem a thorace morbus nascitur, incipit caput sudare, linguaque sit gravior, aut os amarum, aut tonsillae dolent, oscitatio sequitur sine somno et quiete, gravitas corporis, animi dolor, prurigo corporis, brachia manusque intremiscunt, subitoque tussis arida.'—*Ant. Musa ad Maecen.*

p. 55, l. 1711. 'Vitabis vicium, si vomeris sive jejunus, sive post coenam, vel in balneo, plus autem prodest si jejunus bilem ejeceris, eam enim dicimus matrem morborum.'—*Ant. Musa ad Maecen.*

'Succurrendum est prudenter hoc modo, vomitus quam optime fieri potest, post coenam sine repletione, sineque medicamento citari debet: utiles sunt *et* vomitiones ante cibum, quas Graeci Syrmaismos appellant. Oportet autem eum qui sic vomet, radiculas tenueis praesumere, nasturtium, erucam, sinapi, et portulacam, mox aqua tepida superbibita vomere.'—*Diocles.*

'Oportet igitur dimittere de comestione; et uti vomitu: et post vomitum sumere zucharum rosarum cum ligno aloes et masticare, et post comestionem sumere ad magnitudinem unius nucis de electuario enison, quod est confectum ex ligno aloes and causergam.'—*Sec. Sec.*

p. 55, l. 1712. Etiam uti oportet rosato aceto, vino trito, linguam asperam melle fricet, vel mentae folio, reliqua diligenti medico permittenda sunt.'—*Ant. Musa ad Maecen.*

p. 55, l. 1716. A reminiscence of l. 1275.

p. 55, l. 1721. The body being made up of four humours, diseases were caused by these becoming corrupt, or by any one of them being in excess.

p. 55, l. 1722. 'Dionysoon.' Dyanisum, an electuary made of Aloes and Tansy (Lamb. 501). 'Le quele est fait de aloe, galingale, and grasegrun' (Harl. 219). See its composition in *Villanovanus Antidotarium*, fol. 247b. Op. 1520 fo.

p. 55, l. 1726-7. This is not found in the Latin nor in Diocles, but is in the French and in 18 A. vij.

p. 55, l. 1730. In some copies of the *Sec. Sec.* there is a division 'the eyes' instead of this.

p. 55, l. 1734. 'Rednesse in the kne.' 'Genuum dolor, inflatio, rigor.'—*Sec. Sec.* 'þe knees wexe grete' (18 A. vij.).

p. 56, l. 1744. 'Incurret in dolorem juncturarum, & tergi, in fluxum ventris, corruptionem digestionis, & oppilationem epatis.'—*Sec. Sec.*

p. 56, l. 1755. 'Pleni ex cibo modico esse videntur.'—*Diocles.* 'Tepet appetitus.'—*Sec. Sec.*

p. 56, l. 1758. 'Haec vitia sic emendan*tur*; Foenicul*um* et appi*um* vino austero madefacito, vel earum herbarum radices conteres, ex vino ciathis duobus tantundem aquae calidae vel dauci seminis, *et* myrrhae pusillum tritam in vino, ut supra scripsi, et bibe. Vel radices asparagi, vel herbam erraticam, vel serpillum decoque, eam aquam vino mistam bibe.'—*Ant. Musa ad Maecen.*

'Oportet illud qui hoc sentit hoc facere ut herbam accipiat qua dicitur camomilla; et herbam qua dicitur melilotum; et de earum radicibus: ponat radices et herbas in vino albo odorifero; et sumat ex eo quolibet mane.'—*Sec. Sec.*

'Itaque foeniculi apiique radices, vino albo odorato madefacito, atqui huius diluti cyathos duos, mane jejuno singulis diebus propinabis cum aqua dauci, smyrnii, helenij, quodcunque horum habueris, nam omnia proficiunt: adhaec aqua ciceris macerati cum vino idem efficit.'—*Diocles.*

'Il te convient prendre vne herbe appelle apus, et de la graine de fenoil, & de la racine de archemisce, ou dautre herbe appellee achen, & tiacres, & ouec celles herbes met les racins en bon vin blanc, et de ce vin boy chacun matin ouec vu poy de awe et de mel.'—Harl. 219.

p. 56, l. 1760. A marginal note in Harl. 2251 gives 'Archemise=wingwort' (wormwood): 'Apus is smallage' (water-parsley): 'Acheen, sainacle' (sanicle). 'Attracies is blessed thistle.' A Latin MS. reads 'achen, araneg, arraunce.'

p. 56, l. 1765. Same as l. 1618.

p. 56, l. 1766. 'Ita qua sit temperatum cum aqua & melle, et abstineat a nimia comestione.'—*Sec. Sec.*

p. 57, l. 1784. 'Thre' is altered from two in all the texts: for the sake of the verse doubtless.

p. 57, l. 1786. 'Medus vero affirmavit: quod jejuno stomacho prodest multum sumere de granis milii.'—*Sec. Sec.*

p. 57, l. 1788. 'Greek' is an error; it is in the Latin 'Sane Indus indicavit et dixit,' but some copies give the name Sanages the Greek. Cf. Aug. Müller, *Zeitschr. d. deutsch. morgenl. Ges.*, xxxiv. 544.

p. 57, l. 1789. Mylk seems to be a mistake of Burgh's. 18 A. vij. reads: 'who so ete the graynes of whyt mylle fastyng with water cresses;' 'mil blanc' (H rl. 219). Mastursu is then a mistake for nasturtium. Yet Pliny, 25. 8, says: 'Arcades quidem non medicaminibus uti, sed lacte circa ver.' I had proposed another meaning for mastursu from the Arabic.

p. 58, l. 1808. 'Alibi Aurei' was for long a trouble to me. It is simply a mistake. 18 A. vij. has 'who so ete eche morwe of alibi Amei 7 dragmes, and of swete grapis and Reysynes,' &c. The French has no such words; and on turning to the Latin we find 'et qui comedit *quolibet mane* septem dragmas vuae passae bonae dulcedinis,' which makes it clear that the words are misunderstandings of the reading of a contracted Latin text.

p. 58, l. 1809. 'Passa uva est uva sicca solem passa.' Blanchart's *Lexicon*, p. 472. Uva is a gooseberry sometimes.

p. 58, l. 1818. 'Allea, nux, ruta, pira, raffanus, et tyriaca
Haec sunt antidota contra mortale venenum.'—*Sch. Sal.*

Avicenna says that figs, nuts, and rue make a medicine against all poisons. Aristotle quotes the old story about the weasel fighting with the serpent, first eating rue to arm himself against poison, in the *De Animalibus*. Villanova recommends figs, rue, and sweet almonds.

p. 58, l. 1820. This line stands for a chapter of the Latin text, 'de custodia caloris naturalis.'

p. 58, l. 1828. Enlvmyne is an adjective used of blood.

p. 59, l. 1835. A comparison of this line with l. 1827 shows the wide limits writers of the measure allowed themselves.

p. 59, l. 1851. Perch is Burgh's own favourite, since there is no mention of such fish in his texts.

The *Schol. Salern.* says:

'Si pisces molles sunt, magno corpore tolle:
Si pisces duri, parvi sunt plus valituri
Lucius, et perca, saxaulis, et albica, tenca,
Gornus, plagitia, cum carpa, galbio, truca.'

Perch was a favourite in the days of Ausonius. *Edyllium*, IX. 115—

'Nec te delicias mensarum Perca silebo,
Amnigenos inter pisces dignande, marinis.'

p. 59, l. 1853. This seems contrary to experience. The texts only speak
PHILOSOPHERS.

of hard-skinned fish, and besides, the stews were all dead water, and yet there was no objection to the monks eating the fish in them.

p. 60, p. 1868. 'Signa quidem bonarum aquarum sunt haec, levitas, claritas, bonus color; quando facile calescunt et facile frigescunt; in talibus enim delectatur natura.'—*Sec. Sec.*
The six are difficult to make out, and unfortunately 18 A. vij. is defective here.

p. 60, l. 1886. 'Tarage haue of foreyn dyvers sondys': 'quia continent in se particulas terreas.'—*Sec. Sec.*

p. 60, l. 1892. The same as l. 1261.

p. 61, l. 1919. 'Primum vinum valet senibus *et* hominibus abundantibus in humiditate *et* flegmate: nocet vero juvenibus *et* calidis hominibus Primum ergo calefacit *et* liberat a superfluitatibus frigidis et grossis.'—*Sec. Sec.*
'to' should be read in, here. The last clause in l. 1924 does not seem to have much meaning in this connection.

p. 62, l. 1950. The first part of this line refers to the lees at the bottom: 'cujus fex est in fundo depressa.'

p. 62, l. 1956. 'Quia confortat stomachum: calorem corroborat naturalem: juvat digestionem: conservat a corruptione: ducit cibum: decoquit & perducit ipsum purificatum ad omnia mem*b*ris quae reguntur: et decoquit ipsum cibum in eisdem membris, donec convertatur in sanguinem substantialem: tunc ascendit ad cervicem cum calore temperato: reddit caput securum ab infortuitis casibus: insuper cor letificat: colore*m* rubefacit: linguam reddit expeditam: liberat a curis: et hominem facit audacem: et excitat ad omnia appetitum: et multa alia bona facit.'—*Sec. Sec.*

p. 63, l. 1969. A Lydgate line. See Appendix II., 2.

p. 63, l. 1970. 'Linguam reddit expeditam: liberat a curis.'—*Sec. Sec.*

p. 64, l. 1996. This is attributed to Hippocrates in Lamb. 501. In a Latin text: 'Sapiens quidem aristos bonum vinum commendavit ubi dixit: mirum est de homine qualiter potest infirmari vel mori: cujus cibus est panis optimi frumenti, et carnes commendabiles, et potus bonae vitis.' The root idea of this sentiment is in *Galen de san. tu.* I. 12., *de maras.* 2.

p. 64, l. 1997. See l. 1241.

p. 64, l. 2010. 'Et illum qui inebriatur vino ultra modo sumpto: ut abluat se cum aqua calida; et sedeat super flumina curentium aquarum; et habeat salices atque mirtum; et ungere debet corpus suum cum sandalo confecto; et fumigare cum incensis frigidis et odoriferis. Haec est quidem ebrietatis optima medicina.'—*Sec. Sec.*

p. 64, l. 2014. 'Salwys' in apposition to 'wyllwys.' 'Sallies' is still a dialect name for osier willows.

p. 64, l. 2016. Sandal—'Triasendale' (18 A. vij.), an electuary of which the composition may be found in *Villanovanus*, f. 249*b*. Op. Om. 1520 fo.

p. 64, l. 2021-3 represent a chapter 'Quomodo vini potu est derelinquendus.' Eastern medicine lays stress on continuity of habit, and of making gradual changes—here it recommends taking to raisin water, and so on.

p. 64, l. 2023. Here a great gap occurs. The whole of the magic and alchemy comes between this and the next line, which begins Book III. of the *Sec. Sec.*

p. 64, l. 2024. The English version (18 A. vij.) nearest to Burgh's text runs thus: 'Dere sone, rightwisnes may not ben ouyr preysid, for it is of þe propir nature of glorious God, and it is made to sustene all Rewmes for helpe of his servauntis, and rightwisnes owith to kepe the royalle blood, and the richesse of the possessioune of sugetis, and governe hem in alle her nedes; and what lord doth thus, he is in that case like unto God.'

p. 65, l. 2031. A very involved stanza. It means 'Justice, sent from God to his creatures, made of understanding, a sovereign help to obedient subjects, was sent to princes that they might save their subjects from pillage.'

p. 65, l. 2049. 'Et fuit inventum scriptum in uno lapidem in lingua chaldea: quod rex & intellectus sunt fratres alter altero indigens: nec sufficit unus sine reliquo.'—*Sec. Sec.* Burgh's stanza points to a contract between people and king—an idea not in any of the texts.

p. 65, l. 2052. Another gap occurs here in the text Burgh uses. This line begins Book IV. de consiliariis. The Latin advises the king to have five counsellors (like the five senses), and to listen to their advice separately.

p. 66, l. 2087. Burgh it seems had not the signs mentioned in his text. The Latin says: 'fuit ergo genesis in Venere & in Marte in gradu suo existente Geminis cum Libra. Sydera vero contraria et pessima nondum erat orta: ostendit ergo genesis, quod puer futurus erat sapiens, curialis, velocis manus, boni consilii, diligendus a regibus.'—*Sec. Sec.* How Lydgate would have worked this up! I believe the story comes from Ptolemy's Centiloquium, but I have not verified my reference.

p. 66, l. 2092. 'Insight' should be one word.

p. 67, l. 2126. See l. 404.

p. 68, l. 2150. This stanza describing the properties of a good counsellor is out of place here, and should come after l. 2240.

p. 69, l. 2163. Harl. 2251 has in the margin here, 'Parva sunt arma foris, nisi sit consilium domi.'—Cicero [de off. I. xxij.].

p. 69, l. 2164. 'Et in libro cujusdam medorum mandatum est filio suo: fili, necessarium est tibi habere consilium, quoniam unus es in hominibus. Consule ergo illum qui poterit liberare a potentia: et noli parcere inimico: sed quantumcunque poteris, in ipso tuam victoriam manifesta: et in quolibet tempore, cave tibi a potentia inimici.'—*Sec. Sec.*

p. 69, l. 2178. The quotation marks should be on this stanza; it forms part of the Mede's letter.

p. 69, l. 2188. Either of these readings would do; the meaning of the stanza is: 'take counsel; you are not bound to act on it, and you must weigh it well in any case.'

p. 69, l. 2191. The same as l. 1536.

p. 69, l. 2192. This seems to have been a not uncommon fault in 'divine right' kings. 'Sollicite & diligenter moneo & do tibi optimum consilium, nunquam constituas bajulum in regimine loci tui.'—*Sec. Sec.*

p. 70, l. 2203 begins a new chapter in the texts. 'Experienta circa bajulos.'

p. 70, l. 2206. The counsellor would be put in a corner; if he advises the king to spend his own money, he does not honour him sufficiently; on the other hand, if he advises him to take his subjects', he is an enemy—so nothing is left for the counsellor but to offer the king his own money.

p. 70, l. 2212. Burgh had to translate here a curious phrase, which he misunderstands. 'Si ergo inducet te ad stributionem eorum quae sunt in thesauro tuo, et ostendat hoc esse expediens, scias quod nullum caput pretii ponit in te.' *Sec. Sec.* Lamb. 501 translates it, 'wete you þat he puttys yn þe no good lernynge.'

p. 70 l. 2213-4 are not in the text.

p. 70, l. 2221-3. 'Ut pote eligens et volens confusionem sui operis pro tua gloria.'—*Sec. Sec.*

p. 71, l. 2248. The first mark of a good counsellor. l. 2250. The second. The third—good memory, and the fourth—powers of observation, are omitted. l. 2253. The fifth, 'curialis,' &c. l. 2255. The sixth, he should be specially skilled in arithmetic, which is the ground of all science. l. 2256. The seventh. l. 2258. The eighth.

p. 72, l. 2262. The ninth. l. 2264. The tenth. l. 2269. The eleventh. l. 2276. The twelfth. l. 2279. The thirteenth. l. 2281. The fourteenth. l. 2283. The fifteenth.

p. 72, l. 2290. Another chapter begins here. 'Quod homo sit minor mundus.'

p. 73, l. 2299. One cannot account for this line; the text is 'durus et austerus ut coruus,' and all the translations are right. Did Burgh read *cornus*, and make a shot at 'hart,' 'horned animal'?

p. 73, l. 2304. The Latin for 'contagious' is *stolidus*, 'boystous,' 'rude,' in the versions.

p. 73, l. 2305. 'Litel kyng,' 'regulus,' 'parvus rex,' 'rutel.' Fr. 'rambe,' the wren.

'The wren, the wren, the king of all birds,'

is school-boy language all over the world.

p. 73, l. 2311. A favourite phrase of Burgh's. See ll. 1562, 1894.

p. 73, l. 2317. After this comes in the texts a chapter on having servants of the same faith as oneself, with the story of the Jew and the Magian. 'Enchanter of the Orient,' Lamb. 501 calls him. In medieval Europe such advice was needless, and was dropped out in the shorter texts.

p. 73, l. 2318. This begins the fifth book of the *Sec. Sec.*

p. 74, l. 2336-8. Burgh misunderstands his text, which advises the king to make his secretaries feel that their security and prospects depend on his welfare.

p. 74, l. 2339. Beginning of Book VI., 'de nuntiis.'

p. 74, l. 2346. This line seems to be a shot at a translation of a line which the versions omitted: 'quia forte est juxta noctem, et ejus intentio in alio est.' The picture is of the king suddenly calling on one of his lords, charging him with his embassy, and expecting him to set off on the moment. One must leave out the line if one wishes to follow the sense.

p. 75, l. 2358. The king is warned of the Persian custom of making all ambassadors drunk.

p. 75, l. 2367. This seventh book, 'de subditis domus propriae,' seems to refer to the treatment of the king's personal following as distinct from the general body of his subjects.

p. 75, l. 2368. Chaucer is quoting from the *Sec. Sec.* in his *L. of G. W.*, 379, and seq. 390.

'He must thinkin it is his liegeman
As is his tresour, and his golde in cofer
This is the sentence of the philosopher.'

p. 76, l. 2395. The complaint as to Judges being partial is later than the old translations. It is found in 18 A. vij., but not in Lamb. 501.

p. 76, l. 2401. Book 8, 'de ordine & multitudine bellatorum,' with its tale of the wonderful horn figured by Kircher from the Vatican MS., is omitted in 18 A. vij and here. See Lamb. 501 for a translation of it.

This begins book 9: 'de bello.'

p. 76, l. 2404. The semicolon should be at the end of the next line.

p. 78, l. 2456. Burgh uses this metaphor again. See lines 1536 and 2191.

p. 78, l. 2465. This begins book 10 on physiognomy. It has always attracted attention, and of late years has been much studied. I hope to enter in some detail on the connection between this work and the genuine treatises of Polemon and of Aristotle. I am disposed, after some study, to attribute the whole of the remainder of the poem to Lydgate, with perhaps touches by Burgh. There would be more likelihood of this, since in many MSS. this book stands by itself as a separate work, and since it has indeed been printed as such. Sl. 3469 treats the Latin text as a separate work, and the fact of two of our MSS. omitting this part of the poem shows that there was something to mark it off from the rest of Burgh's work. The Envoi is distinctly, as I have elsewhere remarked, Lydgatian.

p. 78, l. 2466. If the remainder is Lydgatian, this stanza seems Burgh's. Compare the line-endings of 2466 and 1581; 2468 and 1539; 2469 and 1525.

p. 78, l. 2473. A Lydgate line, l. 498.

p. 78, l. 2474. A Lydgate line, l. 491.

p. 78, l. 2475. A line Lydgate has taken from Chaucer (*K. T.*, 1086), and used before, l. 500.

p. 78, l. 2476. See l. 501.

p. 78, l. 2479. This is the well-known story of Zopyrus and Socrates. See Cic. de fato, 5, 10. Tusc. IV. 37, 80. Alexand. Aphrod. de fato, 6. Euseb. prep. ev. VI. 9, 22. Polemon was the only writer on physiognomy known to the Arabs, and Socrates is not very different in its Arabic form from Hippocrates, who was far better known.

Some Arabic texts give the name as Aclimas.

p. 79, l. 2493. This stanza is identical with stanza 71, ll. 491-7, with the exception of l. 2499.

p. 80, l. 2518. Hippocrates said that what Philomon had said was true of his disposition, but that he had combatted his nature.

p. 80, l. 2530. 'Fuge ergo ab omni homine livido et flavo quoniam declivis est ad vitia et luxuriam.'—*Sec. Sec.* One of the Hebrew texts adds: 'Inspice tibi Germanos has ultimas proprietates possidentes, scilicet stultitiam, perfidiam, et impudentiam.'

p. 80, l. 2542. 'Cave et precave ab homine infortunato et diminuto in aliquo membro sicut cavendum est ab inimico.'—*Sec. Sec.*

p. 80, l. 2546-8. Not in the text.

p. 81, l. 2556. 'Et raritas verborum nisi cum necesse fuerit, mediocritas in sonoritate vocis et subtilitate.'—*Sec. Sec.*

p. 81, l. 2563. The Latin treats of 'hairs,' but Lydgate (or Burgh) has connected with a sentence on ears in l. 2567: 'Qui habet aures magnas est valde fatuus.' The text for the hair is: 'Capilli autem plani et suaves significant mansuetudinem & frigiditates cerebri: multitudo vero capillorum super utroque humero significat stultitiam et fatuitatem.'

p. 81, l. 2570. This is altogether different from the Latin text. 'Multos etiam habere pilos in ventre et pectore declarat horribilitatem, et singularitatem naturae, et diminutionem apprehensionis, et amorem injuriarum.' Probably our poet allowed his personal knowledge to correct his text.

p. 81, l. 2578. 'Love *of* resoun' would agree better with the texts.

p. 82, l. 2586. 'In-voys,' 'invidus est, inverecundus, piger, inobediens, et precipue si sint lividi.'

p. 82, l. 2590. Insert a comma after curteys.

p. 82, l. 2593. 'Qui vero habet oculos similes oculis asini, insipiens est, et durae naturae.'

p. 82, l. 2600. 'Levyng'; 'fraudulentus, latro, et infidelis.'

p. 82, l. 2611. The Latin is 'significat ineptitudinem (*or* impeditionem) loquendi': 'evyl manere of spekyng.' Lamb. 501.

p. 83, l. 2615. No foundation in text for this.

p. 83, l. 2621. 'Probus et audax.'

p. 83, l. 2623. 'Simus est impetuosus.'

p. 83, l. 2625. 'Valde iracundus.'

p. 83, l. 2628. 'Verbosus et mendax.'

p. 83, l. 2637. 'Of ignoraunce the miste to chace away.'—*C. of L.*, 25.

p. 83, l. 2638. 'Facies plana carens tumorositate (rugis) significat litigiosum, discolum, injuriosum, et immundum.'

p. 83, l. 2644. 'Qui vero habet faciem mediocrem in genis et temporibus vergentem ad pinguedinem: est verax, amans, intelligens, atque sapiens, servitialis bene dispositus ac ingeniosus.'

p. 84, l. 2647. Here should come the passage about the ears, which our poet has transposed.

Grossa vox et sonora significat bellicosus et eloquens.
Mediocris　　　　　　" 　sapiens, providus, verax, justus.
Velox in verbis　　　 " 　improbus, stolidus, importunus, mendax.
Grossa　　　　　　　" 　iracundus et praecipitans, malae naturae.
Dulcis　　　　　　　 " 　invidus et suspitiosus.
Pulchritudo vocis　　 " 　stoliditatem, insipientiam, et magnanimitatem.

p. 84, l. 2660. 'Qui vero habet collum grossum est stolidus, et comestor magnus.'—*Sec. Sec.*

p. 84, l. 2670. 'Elevationes vero humerorum est signum asperitatis naturae, et infidelitatis.'

p. 84, l. 2678. 'Pedes vero carnosi et grossi significant fatuitatem et amorem injuriae.'

p. 85, l. 2680. 'Pedes vero parvi et leves significant audaciam et fortitudinem (aeduritiem).'

p. 85, l. 2682. Largenesse is subject to betokenyth.

p. 85, l. 2684. In knees follows fflessby.

p. 85, l. 2687. 'Steps' should be inserted after 'hath' (without MS. authority). 'Et cui passus sunt breves est impetuosus et suspitiosus, impotens in operibus, & malae voluptatis.'

p. 85, l. 2710. This piece of advice is found in all writers on physiognomy, especially in the ancient ones, such as Aristotle himself, and Rhasis.

Additional Note.

Laud 416 and 673 in the Bodleian have 'pourpartie' for inpartye in l. 160. Ashmole 46 reads as our MS., from which it is probably a copy written by the same hand.

GLOSSARY.

abovyn, 100, 423, above
abrayde, 308, sprang up
accoord, 187, agreement
accordith, 914, 1415, agree
accordaunce, 1357, agreement
acheen, 1760, sanicle
afor, 634 }
aforn, 138, 261, 849, 892 } before
affecyoun, 23, 198, 454, 466, 621, relation to, affection
ageyn, 114 &c. 630, before, and opposite to
aldayes, 2336, 2421, always
amerously, 257, bitterly
apus, 1758, water-parsley
archemise, 1760, wormwood; arthemise would be nearly the correct name for the plant
assayes, 59, 157, tests, trials
atracies, 1760, blessed thistle
attemperaunce, 184, 759, 773, 872, 895, 1246, 1261, temperance, due combination of qualities in correct proportion
atwen, 39, 521, &c. }
atwix, 305, 1099, &c. } between
atwixen, 772, &c. }
avysed, 639 }
avysee, 213 } prudent, foreseeing
avysement,1332, counsel
avyseness, 17, 374, 668, prudence
avys, 154, 176, 183, 902, 1011, 1239, prudence, advice

baas, 2556, low
bolnyth, 1734, swelleth
boote, 1299, repair, remedy
brede, 1133, breadth
brosyd, 1709, bruised, injured
broyde, 737, border
brynstoun, 1648, sulphur
busshement, 2406, ambush

caas, 912, chance
cammyd, 2623, crooked
carpe, 708, say, speak
caste, 153, 516, 2213, reckon
casuel, 911, 927, by chance
celerys, 1439, cellars
ceryously, 352, in series
chawyd, 1713, chewed
cherysshe, 12, 15, 189, &c., hold dear
chevyssh, 2210, procure
claperys, 1321, rabbit-burrows
clours, 1314, 1341, colours
confortatyff, 1717, strengthening
congrew, 1538, congruous
contagious, 1646, 2304, harmful
contirfeet, 404, 2126, manufactured
contvne, 419, continue
counfort, 69, 307, 332, 1150, to strengthen
courbyd, 1417, curved, bent
coveityse, 742, 763, 1042, 2406, covetousness
covennable, 2382, suitable

dar, 355, 538, 923, 1322, 1449, dare
decertys, 1141 }
discertys, 893, 896, 1388, } deserts
declyne, 394, draw off
deffye, 1623, 1833, digest
delyver, 1970, limber, nimble
demenyd, 117, governed, cf. demesne
dempte, 617, deemed
depnesse, 2233, quagmire
dewyd, 99, endued
digne, 33, 135, worthy
discrase, 1213, 1231, to make up one's mind
discure, 726, discover
doon, in Burgh is practically used as we now use the unemphatic 'do,' cf 1635, 1680, 1993, &c.
doun, 996, done

dowmbe, 2310, dumb
dowset, 1683, dulcet, sweet
dragmes, 1808, drachms
dyspayr, dispeyr, 163, 192, 284, in-
 equality

egir, 1707, bitter
empryses, 117, 179, undertakings, 782,
 enterprises
encence, 2019, incense, sweet herbs
enfoorme, 2133, inform, to mould or
 form
enserge, 2472, ensearch, search out
entende, 805, listen
entendement, 63, understanding
equiperacioun, 2367, r. equality
erst, 685, before
euerychoon, 353, 1242 } each
euerych, 565
exordye, 333, exordium
expert, 358, proved
expleyted, 285, filled, completed
explotourys, 2452, *exploratores*, spies

feel, 2307 } fell
fel, 2434
fervence, 248, fervour
fervent, 347, hot
feynt, 866, feigned
flix, 1746, flux
fooly, 897, folly
foltyssh, 581, 775, foolish
foly, 2407, fool-like
forthre, 398, to assist
forthryd, 283, assisted
fourthe, 1670, foremost
foysoun, 1644, abundance

gentillesse, 130, 830, 1180, gentleness,
 nobility
glede, 347, burning coal
gre, 21, will
grees, 1622, grease
grucchyng, 113, 775, 780, 778, grudging
gryffyd, 2373, grafted
guerdownyth, 900, 1390, rewardeth

herborwed, 2084, harboured, lodged,
 entertained
holly, 32, wholly
hovith, 1184, r. behoveth

incondigne, 1532, unworthy, because
 untrained

inpartye, 160. See Notes; if the word
 is read jupartye, it can only be in a
 very extended sense
invoys, 2586, envious
ioweler, 554, jeweller
joye, 2046, enjoy
iupartye, 305, 784, 1113, jeopardy,
 hazard

keep, 1284, 9, 11 } as in housekeeping
kepyng, 799, 957
kynde, 752, nature

large, 749, 857, 917, liberal
largesse, 739, 745, 864, 869, liberality
lecture, 379, 417, reading
lefft, 660, lift
legis, 10, 851, lieges
lepre, 1658, leprosy
lesyng, 1390, 2256, lying
lesyth, 1440, loseth
letuary, 1722, electuary
levene, 705, flash of lightning
levyng, 2600, unbelieving
liges, 851, 853, 917, lieges, subjects
litel, 547 } little
lyte, 762
longanymte, 361, Lat.: *longanimitas*,
 constancy
lukyr, 2398, lucre
lyst, 338, lest, 280, 422, 575, &c., 2021,
 like
lyve, 227, life

massageer, 479, 2341, &c., messenger
mawgre, 156, in spite of
maystryes, 2450 (*magisteria*), works
 showing in them the master's skill
mede, 670, reward, bribe
medle, 522, 548, 552, 837, 847, 898,
 1657, mingle
meenesse, 2533, mediocrity
megre, 265, meagre
mekyl, 763, 1247 } much
mechyl, 1226, r.
mewe, 2062, cage, coop
molte, 1318, melted
morwe, 1807 }
morwen, 1326 } morning
morwening, 1763
motlees, 1378, livery
mowne, 1471, must, should
murily, 1441, ripely, in fitting time
mvt, 1167, 1260, must, ought, 2722,
 (optative) may

Glossary. 121

myshumours, 1922, corrupted humours from whence arose diseases
namely, 385, &c., especially
nevene, 322, name
noblesse, 145, 966, nobility
nyce, 2569, foolish

O, 216, 1164, 1421, one, 445, or
onyment, 2016, ointment
oost, 2421, 2428, host
organycalle, 2095 }
organychall, 2543 } natural
orlogge, 1463, clock, horloge
ostage, 1470, lodging
outrage, 18, 54, 569, excess, conceit
outragious, 572, excessive
outragiously, 1975, superfluously
owmbre, 402, shadow
owylle, 2147, of will

pallith, 1091 }
pallyd, 404 } beats down, weakens
parfight, 273, 365, 386, 1520, perfect
perlees, 260, peerless
pesecoddys, 1374, pease
peyse, 17, 164, 169, 771, 774, 817, 820, 1435, weigh
phisichal, 1803, physical
pistel, 127 }
pistil, 476 r., 637, 652, 659 } letter
plat, 2638, flat
pleyne, 955, border on
polityk, 3, 373, statesmanlike
pondorosite, 1798, weight
poraylle, 810, 1398, O.-F. *pouraille*, poor people
povert, 1384 }
poverte, 934, 1279 } poverty
preef, 183 }
preff, 1632 } proof
preve, 2017 }
prees, 554, 611, a press, a crowd
prenotaryes, 2399, prothonotaries
preperat, 2014, prepared
preys, 910, 920, 1324 }
prys, 215 } praise
processe, 20, 639, 1253, 1380, Lat.: *processus*, narrative. Cf. proses
prohemye, 2169, proëm
provyde, 40, 138, 639, 667, 790, foresee
purslane, 1378, a pot herb, formerly much used, of the genus Portulaca
pyleer, 705, pillar

quarteyn, 1813, quartain, the ague
queme, 202, to please
quyketh, 1299, gives life to

rakyl, 2353, hasty, rash
recurys, 2033, O.-F. *recours*, recourse
reffreytes, 816, springs
rembarbe, 1984, rhubarb
repayer, 287, O.-F. *repairer*, from Lat. *repatriare*, restore to one's country
replesshyd, 1649, 1783, replenished, full
rerage, 571, arrears
resaylle, 2279, receipts
resynges, 1809, raisins
reysed, 705, raised, 1698, received
reyseth, 1932, raiseth
rolle, 2057, enroll
roseet, 1712, roseate
rottle, 1744, ? knee-cap, from L. *rotula*
ryvaylles, 1328, banks

sacryd, 317, consecrated
salwys-wyllwys, 2014, sallow willows, osiers
schent, 1424, break
seece, 175, cease
sekirnesse, 75, security
sewith, 133, followeth
seyn, 127, 547, 625, 1140, seen, 349, 355, 357, 538, 657, say
shokked, 354, stored; cf. shocks of corn
sith, 1210, 1253, 1505, chance
skornys, 2705, gibes, 'flouts and sneers'
slaundre, 1356, slender
sogeer, 1459, sojourn
sondys, 1886, sands
soote, 677, 837, 1300, sweet
sorippys, 1990, syrups
sowdiours, 808, mercenaries
spatlyng, 1416, spitting
stant, 897, 1211, 1799, stand
stewe, 579, fish-pond
stillyng, 1861, distilling in drops
stok, 1943, 2000, 2373, place, body
stynt, 304, stay, stand
sugryd, 220, 376, 882, 889, 1309, sugared, sweetened

tabourerys, 883, drummers
t'abyde, 614, &c., to abide
t'accomplysshe, 182, &c., to accomplish
t'agreen, 468, to agree

tarage, 1886, 2001, ? flavour
tarye, 538, 2302, tarry
t'assaye, 582, to assay
temperat, 1277, 1310, modified, proportioned
t'enlvmyne, 252, 311, 14, to illumine
termyne, 811, to end, to determine
th'answere, 161 r., the answer
th'avys, 118, the advice
thewys, 31, 1071, manners, virtues
t'obeye, 602, to obey
the t'othir, 642, the other
tonne, 249, tun, vessel
tours, 1244, circles
tressyd, 952, 1003, from tress

tretable, 213, 363, 943, 2242, O.-F. *traitable*, tractable

verray, 194, 627, 1098, true

wakir, 227, 381, watchful
warysoun, 2337, 2413, protection, remedy, cure
wayours, 1877, horse-ponds (O.-F. *gayoir*)
wepne, 2415, weapons
wheer, 932, 1419, whether
withseye, 1109, withstand, gainsay
wood, 573, mad
wurschepe, 327, honour

The manufacturer's authorised representative in the EU for product safety is Oxford University Press España S.A. of El Parque Empresarial San Fernando de Henares, Avenida de Castilla, 2 - 28830 Madrid (www.oup.es/en or product.safety@oup.com). OUP España S.A. also acts as importer into Spain of products made by the manufacturer.

Printed and bound by CPI Group (UK) Ltd, Croydon, CR0 4YY

20/03/2026

02075337-0020